HOOKED

HOW CRAFTING
SAVED MY LIFE

by Sutton Foster

GRAND CENTRAL
PUBLISHING
LARGE PRINT

Grand Central Publishing
Hachette Book Group
1290 Avenue the Americas, New York, NY 10104
grandcentralpublishing.com
twitter.com/grandcentralpub

First Edition: October 2021

Grand Central Publishing is a division of Hachette Book Group, Inc. The Grand Central Publishing name and logo is a trademark of Hachette Book Group, Inc.

The publisher is not responsible for websites (or their content) that are not owned by the publisher.

The Hachette Speakers Bureau provides a wide range of authors for speaking events. To find out more, go to www.hachettespeakersbureau.com or call (866) 376-6591.

Print book interior design by Jeff Stiefel.

Library of Congress Control Number: 2021939214

ISBNs: 978-1-5387-3428-5 (hardcover), 978-1-5387-0704-3 (large print), 978-1-5387-0901-6 (Barnes & Noble Black Friday signed edition), 978-1-5387-0840-8 (BN.com signed edition), 978-1-5387-0839-2 (signed edition), 978-1-6388-3033-7 (10-copy ppk signed edition), 978-1-5387-3427-8 (ebook)

Printed in the United States of America

LSC-C

Printing 1, 2021

For Helen and Emily, a couple of Dales

CONTENTS

INTRODUCTION

Get a Hobby

When the Boston Conservatory at Berklee asked me to give the commencement speech to its 2019 graduating class, my answer was an enthusiastic "Yes!" How could I respond in any other way when presented with the opportunity to receive an honorary doctorate from this highly revered music college? This was my *second* honorary degree, as my *first* was from Ball State University, where I am on the theater faculty, which is wild to me, considering I dropped out of Carnegie Mellon after my freshman year. As I sat down to prepare my speech, I thought about what I wished someone had told me when I was the same age as these bright-eyed, hugely talented, and hopeful graduates. What were the principles I turned to again and again when life felt challenging? It didn't take me long to figure out what to say. I boiled it down to three pieces of advice:

Number 1: Say YES.

To any exciting opportunity! However terrifying or beyond your comfort zone. Say yes to life.

Number 2: Trust your gut.

Even if others don't agree. In the end, no matter what happens or how it all turns out, it will have been *your* choice. Own your ...oices, because even if you fail, your gut will get smarter. But if you follow someone else's gut and you fail, all you learn is...to trust your own gut.

Number 3: Get a hobby.

Or two or three! Find a creative outlet. Something that doesn't require someone to give you permission to do it. Pick something that has nothing to do with what you do for a living. And pick something that brings you joy.

This last piece of advice is perhaps the most important, for me at least.

Most people know me as an actress, either as Liza, the forty-year-old divorcée passing as a millennial to get a publishing job on *Younger*, or perhaps as Reno, the tap-dancing evangelist-turned-nightclub-chanteuse in *Anything Goes*. Some know me as a singer and may have even come to my cabaret show at the Café Carlyle. But anyone who knows me well knows that I am as passionate about crafting as I am about singing, dancing, and acting. Ultimately, I see myself as a maker, and crafting is the art of making things—it can be crochet, cross-stitch, drawing, cooking, collaging, or even gardening. It can also be creating a musical, or an evening of song, or a book. What matters most is that there is something tangible at the end of the process. Plus, the very act of making these things is what keeps me centered.

Anxiety runs in my family—in me. I am the daughter of an agoraphobic mother.

I make a living as a performer. It's complicated. And yet, if I am feeling anxious or overwhelmed, I crochet, or collage, or cross-stitch. These hobbies have literally preserved my sanity through some of the darkest periods of my life. So when I thought about writing a book, it seemed like a no-brainer that crafts would play a major role. Each beautiful thing I have made over the years tells the story of who I was when I made it. (Mostly blankets! *Dozens* of blankets!) My crafts have helped hold me together and given me a place to pour all of my love or sadness into.

You'll see in this book that when I talk about crafts, I mean a wide range of things, but I do have a favorite. I first got hooked (get it?) on crochet when I was on a national tour with *Grease*, playing Sandy Dumbrowski. I was nineteen years old and had lost my voice, so I was on a forced two-week vocal rest. I went to stay with my parents, who were living in Memphis, Tennessee, at the time, and since I couldn't speak, I wanted a project to help me pass the time. I went to a craft store, likely Michaels or Jo-Ann

Fabrics, which are now two of my favorite places on the planet, and bought a book called *How to Crochet*. It was New Year's Eve 1994, and I wrote the following entry in my journal: "On this 1st day of 1995, I taught myself how to crochet. I think it's neat. I want to make people things."

Since then, some of my proudest achievements are things I've created with my hands—whether it be the penguin baby blanket I made when my daughter Emily was born or the toilet-paper-roll cover I crocheted for Hilary Duff's wedding present—because what else do you get Hilary Duff but a handmade albino octopus toil-paper-roll cover (with rainbow button suckers on its cream tentacles)?

Most recently, I decided to cross-stitch a Christmas stocking for Emily, similar to one my mother stitched for me when I was a child. My mom and I had a complicated relationship. And while I cannot find that stocking, I still have the Strawberry Short-cake bookmark she made me when I was eight years old. That was during the peak of my obsession with the red-haired cartoon character. I had coloring books, figurines, and even a garbage pail, all store-bought. I find it so moving that my mother took the time to meticulously stitch that sweet girl in her poufy pink bonnet and white frilly apron into existence. She added my first and last name in red thread and a row of hearts in pink and green, then finished the piece with a calico border. I don't recall my mother saying "I love you" often. But I do know that she poured her love for me into that bookmark. I tell my daughter I love her every day. But, following my mom's example, I also make things for her as tangible proof of that love.

Similar to the list of roles I've played on TV or Broadway, I have a hobby résumé. For every production I was in or concert I have sung, there is a collage or stuffed animal that tells the behind-the-scenes backstory of my life. On set, I was making out with Peter Hermann, one of my love interests in *Younger*. In my dressing room, I was crocheting a pink dinosaur for Emily. Every piece I describe within these pages means so much more than the yarn or marker with which it was made. Each is a time capsule and heirloom, spanning my past, present, and future, and together they tell a fuller, more complex and colorful story of who I am and how I want to be remembered.

This is not your traditional memoir. I wanted to root my stories in the things I have made over the years, so the result is an overlapping, not unlike my most recent crafting feat: mosaic crochet. For this, you use two different colors of yarn at a time, switching back and forth often, working into previous rows. It is never straight across — you have to double back to make intricate patterns. The result is layered, colorful, and complex.

I wrote this book for my mother and my daughter. The first so I might better understand her; the second so she might better understand me.

HOOKED

CRAFTING

A Family Affair

People often ask me if music or acting runs in my family, and the answer is no. Not even close! But as it turns out, crafting does. Not in the *Home Sweet Home*, "my mama taught me how to cross-stitch when I was little" way of Norman Rockwell paintings. My mother smoked two packs of cigarettes a day (as did my dad) and never taught me how to make anything, other than a beef Stroganoff using ground beef and Campbell's Cream of Mushroom soup. (More on that later.) But I do have a very clear image of her sitting on the couch of our living rooms in both Athens and Augusta, Georgia—we moved often when

I was young—smoking a Salem menthol, sipping on Pepsi, and cross-stitching. I'm not sure why my mom chose this rather old-fashioned craft as a hobby. Maybe, like getting married and having kids, it was just the thing to do. I wish I could ask her, but she died at the young age of sixty-six— eerily, the same age as her mother, Lenora, from whom I got my middle name. Lenora did intricate stitching called "tatting" on handkerchiefs and linen, and my Aunt Mary Anne, my mother's older sister, is an incredible knitter and crocheter and cook. My mother liked to cross-stitch. I crochet.

I know this is all connected somehow. It's why I wanted to write this book: I am looking for the common thread.

My mother, Helen Dale Jackson, grew up in a one-light town in North Carolina called Chadbourn. According to my Aunt Mary Anne, she was a social person and had a circle of friends in which, at times, she was even considered a ringleader. She could be bossy and an instigator, but there were no signs of the agoraphobia that so incapacitated her later in life. Her dad, an intimidating man whom we called Dada, was once the mayor of Chadbourn. He also owned the local department store, Jackson's, which sold everything from clothing to housewares to furniture and fabric. Dada was known to be downright mean—and he was a millionaire! That was how my parents described him, and how I remember him. We visited him every summer during my childhood at one of his many houses (lake, river, *and* beach). When I close my eyes, I see him in his light-yellow Cadillac, wearing multiple gold chains. He was not warm and fuzzy. He believed children should be seen and not heard. My Aunt Mary Anne told me that growing up in Dada's house, his children knew to do what he told them to do. He had a temper. In short, he lived up to his reputation.

My mother was nineteen years old when she told Dada that she wanted to move to New York to become a model. She was rail thin, like Twiggy, and would accompany her father when he traveled through the South to meet with dress manufacturers. Sometimes, they would go to fashion shows together. As she watched those women strut down the runway, a seed was planted in her that Dada squelched immediately, saying, "Absolutely not." Instead, she went to community college, where she met my father. They fell in love, and when my mother told her father she wanted to marry him, Dada forbade that as well. That was too much. My mother clearly wanted control of her life, so she eloped. The story goes that when my mother shared the news with her father, his response was, "Are there any more surprises?" (Hunter, my brother, arrived a year and a half later, by the way.)

Marrying my father set my mother apart from her tight-knit family. She defied Dada, which no one else dared to do, first by eloping, then by being the only family member to leave her home state. After Hunter was born in Lumberton, North Carolina, my dad, a regional car salesman, was transferred to Statesboro, Georgia, where I was born six years later. We moved to Athens when I was five, and I have two distinct memories of that house: that our backyard had honeysuckle and blackberry bushes, and that our street was called Knob Lick Drive, which I still find hilarious. (I mean, *come on.*) I also remember riding my Big Wheel up and down the street until my mom made me sell it at our garage sale. She said I had outgrown it—I disagreed and was furious. She won, as would be the pattern for most of my young life.

My mom could be harsh, but she was also very funny, often both at once. She's the source of the family legend that said I was bought at Kmart sitting between Godzilla and King Kong. Any time I misbehaved, my mom would threaten to send me back to the store. It worked, because I believed her. She also told me she had lizards in her purse to keep me from going near it. And that if I ate a grape seed, a plant would grow inside my stomach and out of my nose. I accidentally swallowed a seed one afternoon at school and panicked. I was so upset that the nurse sent me home, and I was too ashamed to tell my mother what had happened. I waited for days and weeks for that tree to grow! (I'm happy to report that it's been over forty years since this incident and I am still tree-free.)

When I was in my twenties, I discovered a snapshot of Hunter as a child, dressed up in a housecoat, wearing a wig and glasses. He called this character "Bobo." I asked my mom about it, and she clarified that it was in fact *her* costume.

"I would dress up in disguise when you were a toddler," she explained in a matter-of-fact way.

"Why?" I asked.

"So you wouldn't recognize me," she said.

"What?" I was dumbfounded.

"I was stuck at home with two kids," she said. "And you wouldn't leave me alone. You were annoying."

I was a toddler and have no memory of this at all, but it definitely tracks.

My mother enrolled me in ballet class at age four. She had taken dance lessons as a child as well, so she thought it was the right thing to do. But she also believed that it would help focus me, my dad recently explained. Apparently, I was "too energetic," he said. And I ran into things.

According to him, I almost missed out on my first brush with musical theater because of this boundless childhood energy. Hunter had gotten the part of Linus in a local production of *You're a Good Man, Charlie Brown* being performed at our church in Statesboro. My parents were nervous about bringing me to the rehearsal since I had such a hard time sitting still. I'm grateful they took the chance, because I will never forget seeing my big brother up there on that small stage, singing his heart out. I was so mesmerized—I wanted to do *that*. The pull was magnetic. It looked *fun*.

The story goes that I didn't move for the entire run-through, and this left such an impression on my parents—especially my mother—that, soon after, she started looking for similar opportunities for me. This was the beginning of my mother living her own unrealized dreams through her children.

In Augusta, she found a local theater company, the Augusta Players, for both me and Hunter. My first time onstage was in their production of *A Christmas Carol*. My mom also found the Augusta West Dance Studio, where I started taking jazz and tap in addition to ballet. I was very good at following directions and wanted to do everything right, so my teacher put me front and center for our first performance. It was the first time in my life I received applause, and it will not surprise you to hear that was a standout moment for me: I was like, *What is this fabulousness?* I was hooked. And my parents were, too. They were always in the audience with flowers or a balloon, so proud.

I started experimenting with humor on the stage from the start. My dance studio did a holiday show where I was cast as an elf. I wore a green-and-red suit and curly-toed shoes that had bells on them. My job was to open a giant box that released toy soldiers. The first time I did it in front of the audience, I fell down when I opened the box—on a whim. The audience gasped, and then erupted in laughter when they realized that I had done it on purpose. I credit Carol Burnett for inspiring me with her physical comedy—my family watched her variety show religiously, and I identi-fied with her. I was the tallest girl in my dance class, and she was a goofy, funny, tall clown! In another performance of that pageant, I pretended to struggle to get the lid off, which got a lot of laughs as well. I soaked it up! These were my first memories of cause and effect. I do this, and the audience responds. I have been using humor in my performances ever since.

My mother saw how comfortable I was on the stage and continued to seek out more ways to support the spark she saw. I was ten years old when she spotted the flyer for a production of *Annie* at the Augusta Players. They were casting the orphans and looking for child actors who could dance *and* sing. The auditions were that same day.

"I think you should try out," my mother suggested.

"What do I have to do?" I asked.

"Just go sing a song," my mother said.

I had never sung in public before, but music had always been a huge part of my life. There was always a record spinning or an eight-track playing in my household: John Denver, the Bee Gees, the Beach Boys, James Taylor, and Dan Fogelberg were in constant rotation. Hunter, who was sixteen, took it further by forming a parody band called Hunter Jackson and the Knights of Jam, inspired by Weird Al Yankovic. (He loved Michael Jackson, so it was only fitting that he used our mother's maiden name, Jackson, for his rock 'n' roll persona.) So I was exposed to music, but I had no training whatsoever. That said, I had seen the *Annie* movie, with Carol Burnett as Miss Hannigan. I knew and loved all the songs, and would sing "It's a Hard-Knock Life" and "Tomorrow" in the tub, using a hairbrush as my microphone while I belted at the top of my lungs.

I was torn, though: my friend Bethany had just come over for a playdate.

"Bethany can audition, too," my mother suggested.

It was late summer, and I was dressed accordingly in cutoff jean shorts, jelly shoes, and a fringed T-shirt with *Myrtle Beach* spray-painted on it in neon colors. Bethany said she thought it sounded fun, so we all piled into the car.

The theater looked more like a barn.

There was a small stage at the bottom of two sets of risers. After my mother signed us in, Bethany and I followed her toward the top tier.

There were roughly eighty girls auditioning that day. A man called out names from a clipboard and I watched as one girl after the next walked down to a spot near the piano. The director asked each girl to sing a few bars of "Maybe." I knew the song from the movie but had not prepared it. Still, as I listened to each girl sing, I thought, *I can do that.*

The director called my name. As I got up from my seat, my mother said, "Sutton, when you're down there on the stage, make sure to sing up to me, so I can hear you."

I didn't know she sat in the back row on purpose—my Aunt Mary Anne told me this years later.

"And don't forget to smile," she said. This was something both my parents often reminded me to do.

"Yes, ma'am!" I may have said, and then walked down the risers and took my place by the piano. I wasn't nervous at all—it felt like the most natural thing in the world.

The pianist played the intro chords and nodded at me when it was time for me to sing: "Maybe far away! Or maybe real nearby."

I noticed that all the chatter stopped and the room got really quiet—and remained so as I sang through the entire song. When it was over, the silence followed me back up the risers. Everyone was just staring at me, including my mother. She looked pleasantly surprised, not by my performance but by the room's response.

As I took my seat next to Bethany, I asked, "How did I do?"

Her eyes were wide as she squealed, "You were amazing! I had no idea you could sing!"

Bethany auditioned as well but did not get a callback.

Later that evening, my mom told me that I had—for the role of Annie. I knew I should have been excited, but when I first heard the news I was disappointed, because I'd had my heart set on playing Pepper, the tough, sassy orphan. I wasn't sure I wanted to play the lead role.

She said they wanted me to sing "Tomorrow" at the callback.

"You need to practice, Sutton," she said.

Over the next few days, I sang along with the soundtrack, in our living room, standing on the cheese crate on which my father's mother, Maw Maw, had lovingly stenciled the word *Mommy*, her gift to my parents when Hunter was born. (See? I told you crafting ran in the family!) That cheese crate became a de facto stage for so many of my childhood performances. I loved hitting the high notes and belting: "To-MOR-row, to-MOR-row! I love ya, tomorrow!"

My mom sat on the couch and gave notes:

"Sing to the back row."

"Make sure to smile."

"Raise your right arm up on the last note."

She also made me sing it over and over until I got it just right.

It worked. I got the part—and wound up being interviewed on local TV as a result.

"Have you any plans to go into the theater as a profession later on?" the reporter asked me.

"Maybe just a little," I replied.

I had no idea that being onstage and singing could be a profession. I just thought it was something you did for fun.

That was when the musical theater seed took root. Not just for me, but for my entire family. It was something we all loved, and it brought us together. Hunter had natural talent too. He was cast in *Godspell* and then did *Bye Bye Birdie* at his high school, followed by *Joseph and the Amazing Technicolor Dreamcoat*. We both auditioned for the Augusta Players' *The Sound of Music*: I played Brigitta and he played Rolf. My dad bought a giant video recorder to film our performances. (He still has *all* the VHS tapes.) We would host cast parties at our house, eating pizza and drinking Pepsi, those grainy tapes playing in the background. My parents enjoyed it as much as Hunter and I did.

When the director of the Augusta Players asked for help building the set for a production of *Jack and the Beanstalk*, my father volunteered. He was incredibly handy and was always fixing something around the house and in our garage. For the play, he fashioned a twenty-foot vine the width of a fat tree trunk out of chicken wire and green fabric, complete with offshoots. In the production of *Grease*, Hunter was cast as Danny Zuko and I played Patty Simcox, the obnoxious cheerleader. For that, my father salvaged two fenders off a VW he found at the junkyard, and four old tires. He took it all to Milton Ruben Chevrolet, where he welded several pieces of sheet metal together to fashion a car frame that he painted cherry red and slipped on top of a golf cart. That was Greased Lightnin'.

He was very much that dad.

When I think back to my childhood, I see how theater was the happy glue that kept us connected.

But not for long.

TOMATO PLANTS

I have no idea what my parents' anniversary date is. Growing up, I never heard any mention of their wedding or even saw a photo of that day. I also never remember them holding hands, never mind kissing. I didn't think anything of it then—it's just the way things were. As a kid, you don't question your parents' relationship.

We moved to Augusta when I was seven, and I consider that period our golden years. My father was a district sales manager for Chevrolet by then. He drove a giant ice-blue Monte Carlo with a single front bench and back seats without seat belts. Our house had wall-to-wall cream carpeting, an intercom system, and a vacuum that was attached to the wall. I loved that house, and that car, and I often wonder if that's because I associate them with a time when everyone in my family seemed happy.

Every spring, our front yard erupted in bursts of orange and yellow marigolds and daffodils against a hot-pink azalea background. The garden was my dad's great joy, a hobby he looked forward to each year, and I loved helping him plant the marigolds from seed. My mother loved them too, and what I didn't know until I began writing this book was that she would harvest the seeds in the fall from the plants my father had grown the spring before. (If you pop the head off a marigold, all the seeds are in the pod at the base of the bloom.) She'd collect these seeds in small packets and dry them over the winter so they'd be ready to plant the next spring.

My dad would dig a small trench in the narrow garden beds that lined the walkway up to our front door, and then I would sprinkle the seeds down the center and cover them with earth before watering them in. I loved watching the green shoots poke their way through the soil, followed by a sturdy stem and finally a blast of sunshiny orange or yellow blooms. It was a thrilling payoff for this annual ritual.

My dad kept a garden in our backyard, too. There, he planted beefsteak tomatoes, as my mother's favorite meal was a tomato sandwich made with two pieces of soft white bread, a slather of mayonnaise, and a sprinkle of salt. When I close my eyes, I can see the row of tomatoes sitting on the windowsill waiting to ripen. Most summers, he also experimented with green peppers, corn, okra, and sometimes sunflowers—a smaller version of the garden his parents, my Maw Maw and Paw Paw, grew in their backyard. Traditions passed down. But tomatoes were a staple, and his goal was to grow them big enough so one fat slice covered the entire piece of bread.

My mother was a picky eater, but she loved those tomato sandwiches. She was worried about the pesticides my dad used to keep the bugs at bay, so she would peel the tomato before eating it. I never thought much of it then, but like the missing wedding photos, these were all tiny clues about who my mother was and perhaps harbingers of things to come.

I was in sixth grade when things in my family took a dark turn. I can pinpoint the moment.

Bethany and I were still close friends, and she invited me for a sleepover. My mom didn't like me going to other people's homes, even for playdates. She never explained why. But looking back, I now realize that she didn't see the value in nurturing these friendships because she didn't have any friends beyond my Aunt Mary Anne, whom she spoke to on the phone weekly. I can't recall my parents ever going out to dinner with other couples, or my mom even having coffee with a neighbor. So it was always a battle whenever I asked to hang out with my friends. But on this night, I was determined. I marched into her room and was stunned to see her sitting cross-legged on top of her neatly made bed, sobbing.

I had never seen her cry.

"Mommy?" I said.

She turned to me, tears streaming down

her face, and said quietly, "He doesn't love me anymore."

I had no idea what she was talking about.

"Your father is going to leave me," she said, her eyes puffy and red.

I didn't know how to respond, so I said, "Bethany invited me to sleep over."

She started shaking her head and crying even harder. "Don't go! Stay with me!"

I was so caught off guard that I just ignored the bizarre behavior and asked, "Can I spend the night at Bethany's?" I remember feeling paralyzed watching her come undone.

"Stay with me," she pleaded. "Don't go. Daddy doesn't love me."

I suddenly felt claustrophobic. All the air had been sucked out of that bedroom, and I just wanted to run. I quickly slipped out of her room and went straight to Bethany's.

When I came home the following morning, I saw blankets and sheets left on the couch and my mother drinking coffee and smoking a cigarette at the kitchen table. My father was mowing the lawn. The crying incident was never talked about again.

From then on, my dad started sleeping on the couch. And I began to notice that my mom would pick fights with him over the smallest things, like not taking out the garbage or scraping his plate while he was eating. She complained about the *one* beer he drank on Saturdays while he grilled. It was so petty and mean. Her rage so dwarfed any offense that I started defending my dad, and then she would get mad at me.

"Sutton, stay out of this!" she would say, and then storm out of the room.

Even worse, she started to ice me out. I would walk into the room and ask her a question or say hello. She would completely ignore me, as if I weren't standing there in front of her.

Things were fracturing inside our house. The silence was both suffocating and confusing. The nights of pizza parties and balloon bouquets were evaporating. Our family was coming undone, and I had no idea why. No one ever sat me down and said, "We're having a hard time. This is not about you."

At school, Tracy Duffy was my best friend. Or so I thought. At the end of sixth grade, she started becoming friends with another girl and ignoring me. It was more than I could handle. One day at recess, all the stress and frustration I was feeling at home erupted into a torrent of profanity, all aimed at Tracy. I didn't say it to Tracy's face, I just went temporarily mental to another group of girls. I used pretty much every swear word I knew at the time, which probably wasn't extensive — perhaps a few "God damns" and maybe a "fuck" — but for me that was outrageous! Word got back to Tracy, and some of her friends turned me in to the teachers, which was how I ended up in the principal's office.

This was a first for me. The principal was both disappointed and surprised — I was a straight-A student and a goody two-shoes. And I was so mad and hurt that I didn't even care. My home life was a disaster and my best friend was ditching me for someone else. I was thirteen years old and pissed off. The school called my parents, who were mortified, but no one connected any dots. I wasn't even grounded. Once again, it was literally never talked about.

That June, I finished sixth grade, Hunter

graduated from high school, and a month later, we moved to Detroit. My dad was being transferred again, this time to the General Motors headquarters as part of a cost-saving company downsize. But I didn't understand that then. My parents never sat me down to explain what was happening, and so in my prepubescent wisdom, I thought we were moving because I was a difficult and socially awkward kid who was getting in trouble at school.

Everything changed in Michigan. My parents never shared a bedroom again. My mother stopped driving, and complained bitterly about the cold. She also had a real disdain for Northerners, whom she called Yankees. The word seemed to hurt her mouth when she said it, which was often. Over the next six years we lived there, if my mom wanted to be really mean, she'd say to me, "You're a Yankee now." I found that so confusing. *You brought me here!* I'd think. *And also, what does that even mean?*

I tried to talk to someone. In middle school, I made an appointment with one of the school's counselors, not realizing they were hired to help students with their academic workload, not personal problems at home. The counselor just seemed confused.

"I'm not a therapist," she said.

I was disappointed, and desperate for guidance.

And then she asked, "What makes you happy?"

"Performing," I may have answered, as I already knew that the stage was the one place that made sense to me.

Hunter went to the University of Michigan to study musical theater, and I continued to perform as well—both in community theater groups and in high school too. My parents continued to come see us in every show, and tape record the rehearsals, too. When I asked my dad about this period in our lives, he said, "Y'all were our entertainment."

But something had shifted.

When I think back on this time, I now realize it was when my mom stopped cross-stitching and my dad stopped growing things—even tomato plants. All that energy went into finding opportunities for me, in particular, to perform.

PAPA BOB'S TIPS FOR GROWING THE PERFECT TOMATO

My dad didn't have a garden in Detroit—it was too cold for tomatoes, he said. It would take years before he started growing things again. He has a garden now, and we grow tomatoes together. Here are his tips for the perfect sandwich-size fruit.

1. Start with rich, loose soil. Big Yellow Bag Black Garden Soil is fantastic!
2. Find a location with four to six hours of sunlight every day.
3. Beefsteak tomato seeds are best, though Better Boy will also do.
4. Apply Miracle-Gro liquid fertilizer every two weeks, according to directions.
5. Don't overwater.
6. Use tomato cages or supports to help the plants grow *up*. Use twine or yarn to tie the vines to the cages.

7. Watch for bugs. Marigolds planted nearby are supposed to double as insect repellent.

8. Paw Paw used to say, for the perfect tomato, remove all the "suckers," or extra growth shoots, so all the energy gets concentrated into the main vines.

9. Pick the tomatoes when they're near ripe but not quite ripe, so others can grow.

10. Place the picked tomatoes in a sunny spot in your kitchen to let them fully ripen.

BASKET CASE

It was happening again.

I was at rehearsal when Mary Ruvolo tapped me on the shoulder and said, sheepishly, that Trisha didn't want me to watch her.

"Excuse me?" I said, confused. I was nineteen years old and had just joined the national tour of *Grease* in San Francisco. Trisha played Sandy Dumbrowski, and I was her understudy. My job *was* to watch her.

"Or even look at her," Mary added. "I'm sorry. I feel bad about telling you this, but you're driving Trisha crazy."

I could feel my chest tighten. I knew

Mary was simply a pawn in the mean-girl game of telephone that was happening.

I also realized at that moment that I had two choices:

(A) Try to ingratiate myself to Trisha and protect myself from the new-girl hazing that felt certain to follow.

(B) Find another way to contain the anxious feeling now coursing throughout my body.

I knew from experience that A would not work. And so, in order to survive the tour, I needed something to do that would ground me. Something that had nothing to do with the show or its social politics. Something that I could be in complete control of. That was how I started to cross-stitch. I call it my gateway craft.

It's funny, because I always thought of cross-stitch as my mom's hobby. Over the years following my family's move to Detroit, my mother's social anxiety began taking hold of her. She left the house less and less, and as she retreated, her bitterness seemed to grow. Cross-stitch was one of the few things I had ever seen her really enjoy.

I'm not exactly sure why I chose such an antiquated art form, other than that it was a connection to a happier time in my youth — and a happier version of my mother. So instead of trying to insinuate myself into any of the cliques that had formed on the tour, I decided to teach myself how to cross-stitch.

It was a form of self-protection: *I don't need to socialize! I have a project to work on!*

That was my thinking as I went to Jo-Ann Fabrics one afternoon in search of a cross-stitch pattern book. I decided to make my mother a Christmas gift and chose a scene that had three Victorian houses, side by side, each with a wreath on its door and smoke curlicuing out of its chimney. The instructions called for the houses to be a cranberry red and the wreaths, garlands, and pine trees a vibrant hunter green. While others in the cast went out for drinks after the show or went bowling on our days off, I went back to my room, excited: I had something else to do that gave me a purpose beyond performing.

I didn't know then what a profound

impact this would have on me throughout my career.

With cross-stitch, you start in the middle of the fabric and work outward in concentric circles. This ensures that you don't run out of space. Some of my most content moments from that tour were sitting cross-legged on my hotel bed, watching *Days of Our Lives*, poking and pulling my needle through a panel of linen kept taut by an embroidery hoop. With each red *x* I made, slowly but surely, a double-hung window emerged, followed by a shutter, then a shingle, then a door. It was thrilling! And addictive. Not only was I cross-stitching obsessively during my off time, but I started doing it in between shows as well. In hotels, in dressing rooms, and on airplanes. I saw how having a hobby gave me something to do other than obsess about the social dynamics around me. The more I cross-stitched, the less I cared what other people thought about me. I knew that was important. I didn't want to end up in the emergency room *again*.

Two years earlier, when I was seventeen years old, I had joined *The Will Rogers*

Follies national tour. This meant skipping my senior year of high school to travel with a group of virtual strangers—some of them gals twice my age, several of whom were Broadway veterans and one of whom had even worked as a *real* showgirl in Vegas! This was mind-blowing to me, as my nearest brush with anything even close to "professional" had been losing to a thirteen-year-old Richard Blake on *Star Search* and making the final round of auditions for the 1989 reboot of *The Mickey Mouse Club*. (I didn't get the part because I was too old and too tall to be a Mouseketeer.)

I still can't believe my mother let me go. Even though I was deemed too mature for Disney, I'm astonished that I made the cut as a sexy Follies girl. I was so young and in-experienced! To give you a sense of just how sheltered I was at that time in my life:

1. I considered the fettuccine Alfredo at TGI Friday's exotic.
2. My first airplane flight was to Los Angeles for that Mouseketeers audition.

3. I had only ever been away from home without my parents once, and that was the time I spent a week with my Aunt Mary Anne when my dad took my mom to Hawaii. He won the trip at work, and that was the only time they ever took a vacation without me and Hunter. (It was on that visit that Mary Anne taught me to knit, which clearly planted a seed.)

4. I'd had a babysitter exactly once in my life. The story goes that when my parents came home from their night out, the sitter reported that I had tried to put my finger in a socket, and my mother never trusted anyone to watch me again.

And yet my insular and overprotective mother was the one who not only found the audition for me but also told me to lie about my age when the *Will Rogers* casting call came through Detroit in the spring of 1992. They were looking for new, undiscovered talent, and were hosting a nationwide search. The flyer specifically said you had to be eighteen, and I had only just turned seventeen that March. My mother insisted that we should go anyway. After I did a tap number from "Will-a-Mania," the show's opening number, and sang "I'm Not at All in Love" from *The Pajama Game*, Jeff Calhoun, the assistant choreographer to Tommy Tune, approached me and asked, "How old are you?"

"I'll be eighteen on my next birthday," I said, as my mother had specifically instructed me. While I wasn't technically lying, my heart began pounding beneath my leotard in anticipation of a clarifying question.

"Keep tapping, and we'll see you in New York," he said with a smile.

I made it through that second round of Manhattan auditions, and the next thing I knew, I was packing two brand-new turquoise Samsonite suitcases that my parents had bought me to go on this yearlong work trip. I had no clue what I might need "on the road," so I made sure to bring all the essentials: my stuffed gorilla, my special pillowcase, and seven boxes of tampons I asked my mother to buy for me because I had never bought them on my own and wanted to delay that responsibility for as long as possible.

That summer, as all my friends were getting ready to start their senior year, I had to ask my principal for permission to skip it. I only had two credits left to graduate, so he agreed and arranged for me to complete them through correspondence courses. My drama teacher, Mr. Rick Bodick, agreed to oversee one, in which I would read plays and write reports on them. Mrs. Clark, my speech teacher, set up a series of school visits in which I would go speak to local high schools throughout the tour, in the cities where we would perform, about my life on the road. It sounded way more exciting than sitting in class, but I was still sad to miss *West Side Story*, our senior musical that year. Prom? Not so much.

My parents dropped me off at the Hotel Esplanade, an apartment building turned temporary resident housing on the Upper

West Side of Manhattan where most of the *Will Rogers* touring cast was being put up during the five-week rehearsal. I was assigned a one-bedroom suite with two roommates: Wendy Leahy was blond and from Ohio. Wendy Palmer had short, sassy brown hair and, I soon learned, a boyfriend. Both were in their midtwenties. Neither had packed a stuffed animal.

Rehearsals were at the Nederlander Theatre on West Forty-First Street, and my first challenge was getting there. My mother had warned me about the subway. That was where Midwestern girls got raped and murdered! She also told me *never* to walk in Central Park. More rape and murder. Mind you, on her deathbed, my mother cautioned me about air conditioners falling out of New York City windows: "Be careful! Always look up!" Oh, and when I bought a car in my twenties, it was, "Don't drive in the rain. Ever." And, "Never pass a semi truck on the highway! They can't see you in their blind spot." Everything seemed to lead to a premature death. And so rather than risk that on the 1/2/3 train, I walked to and

from rehearsal every day, stopping for a Hot
& Crusty bagel on my way. Buying my own
breakfast made me feel independent, even
empowered—until I hit the mid-Forties
and started passing all the peep shows and
sketchy characters smoking and drinking
from paper bags outside of them. That was
when my mother's voice started up in my
head—again with the rape and murder. But
then I also saw all the theater marquees
with the titles of Broadway shows whose
cast albums I owned back home: *Miss
Saigon! The Secret Garden! Les Misérables!*
The thrill was bigger than the fear.

To add to that excitement, the legendary Tommy Tune, who both directed and
choreographed the show, was at those early
rehearsals, as was Jeff Calhoun. I had just
come from starring as Guenevere in my
junior year production of *Camelot,* and now
here I was doing warm-up yoga (having no
idea what that was or meant) with the entire
cast on our first day of rehearsal. It was all a
little surreal.

I learned fast that I was in over my head
when it came to maturity and experience

offstage, too. That very first week, Wendy P. invited her boyfriend to our apartment. I kept waiting for him to leave. Instead, Wendy announced, "We'll take the living room sofa bed." I was mortified and waited for Wendy L. to be outraged as well. Instead, she lay on her double bed, flipping through *Cosmo*, completely unfazed. I quickly changed into my nightgown and slipped into my bed with my stuffed gorilla, thinking, *OMG, they're going to have sex!* I hadn't even gotten to second base with my high school boyfriend Chris Kuechenmeister, who was the Will Parker to my Ado Annie in my tenth-grade production of *Oklahoma!* I don't think we had even French-kissed, and we most certainly *never* talked about sex. There was no health education at our high school, so when I heard someone mention the word "orgasm" at school one day, I went home and asked my mom, "What is an orgasm?"

"Ask your father," she said, a bit taken aback.

I found him watching football in the den. "Dad, what is an orgasm?"

He stared at me, then back to the TV.

"Ask your mother."

I tried another tactic.

"Does it have to do with sex?" I asked my mom.

"Sutton," my mother said, with a frustrated, dismissive wave, "sex is bad. That's all you need to know."

Following this conversation (if you could call it that), she bought me a book about Christianity and sex, which made it crystal clear that it was a sin to have sex before marriage. I was raised Presbyterian, but we only ever went to church on Easter and Christmas. However, my best friend at the time was a devout Christian. I knew that she was "saving herself" for her wedding night. I devoured the book, which, P.S., also claimed that masturbation was *really* bad, because it would distract you from your relationship. I had questions, like "What the hell is masturbation?," but I knew better than to ask my mom.

Meanwhile, Wendy P. was likely doing *both* in the living room with her boyfriend, and I thought it was scandalous. And yet,

I was playing a Follies showgirl! My character dressed in bustiers and garter belts, no less (or rather, not much more!). Talk about bad casting. In two numbers, I wore powder puffs over my boobs. In another, I wore a cow-patterned unitard and horns on my head; swinging my tail was key to the choreography. No one else in the company seemed to mind these racy and suggestive outfits or moves, but I was gobsmacked by the number of butt cheeks and boobs I saw onstage—and off.

All eighteen Follies gals shared a dressing room, and there were these two gorgeous women, Paulette and Lisa, who would strip naked and keep talking as if they were not naked. I'd avert my eyes and try not to blush. The only other boobies I had seen were in the movies. But I was also fascinated. I had never been around so many strong, confident, sexual women.

After five weeks of rehearsals, we all flew to San Francisco for the first leg of the tour that would take me to twenty-seven different cities over the next twelve months. Even more exciting: during the New York rehearsals, out of the eighteen girls, I was selected to be one of the "six single sisters," which was considered a special role because we had extra numbers and costumes. The strongest singers were chosen, so that was a huge confidence boost. I was out of my element in so many other ways, but I could hold my own onstage. That made me feel like I was making a good impression and getting recognized for my talent. What I didn't realize was that it also made me a target.

Julie Lamar was another single sister. She was a dimpled blonde with a Cheshire cat smile that could crack a mirror, and she would always show up to rehearsals in a thong leotard and fishnet stockings. Julie was *the* cool girl on the tour—a married professional Vegas dancer! For a number called "Our Favorite Son," we wore red-white-and-blue bustiers, garter belts, and hats that doubled as tambourines. Julie sat right next to Keith Carradine, who played Will Rogers, and I was placed next to her, with my hair dyed auburn for symmetry— the girl on the other side of Keith was a tall blonde like Julie, and next to her was a slightly shorter reddish-brunette. It was my favorite number in the show, and I always gave it 150 percent. I thought I was doing really well until a couple of weeks into the tour, when the stage manager pulled me aside and said, "We're going to change the positions in the 'Favorite Son' number. Victoria Waggoner is going to swap places with you."

"Okay," I said, confused.

Every other girl down the line did the opposite choreography from the girls next to her: A, B, A, B, and so on. This meant that I had to learn the opposite choreography from what I had been doing, as did Victoria. No one really explained the change. Victoria and I just had to be at rehearsal the next day to learn each other's parts.

That same afternoon, I was just about to walk into the dressing room when I overheard one of the other girls ask Victoria, "What's up with the switch?"

I stopped short of the door so they couldn't see me.

Victoria shrugged and said, "Apparently,

Julie complained that Sutton was too energetic."

Someone else, I don't know who, laughed.
"Ha! Of course."

That felt like a slap in the face. I had
a hunch Julie didn't like me. More than
once during rehearsals, she'd said, "Stop
being such a spaz, Sutton!" This was always
in front of other girls, who would laugh or
roll their eyes. She'd also complained about
my volume. (I can project!) I had not yet
learned how to control my voice, so each
dig hurt my feelings. I had no idea how
to respond to the comment, other than to
dance with less enthusiasm, to sing with
less volume. To tone it down. Make myself
a bit smaller. Knowing she had specifically
requested for me to be moved away from
her was devastating, really. I felt so out of
my league—I was a senior in high school,
used to getting accolades from my peers. I
started thinking maybe I had made a mistake. Maybe I should go back to high school
and finish out my senior year with my
friends and peers. Auditions for the school
musical would be soon. Maybe I would get

cast. But quitting did not feel like an option. I kept hearing my mom and dad's advice whenever things got hard: "Stay sweet" and "Keep smiling."

So that's what I tried to do.

Not long after that change in the number, I noticed that cliques had begun to form. I have since learned that this can happen on a tour: there is the diva, who holds court, and she picks on the newbie. It felt like a hazing. I would come bounding into a dressing room with my seafoam-green Caboodles makeup case and Sweet Valley High novels, brimming with energy and volume, and would be greeted with annoyed glances or turned heads. Julie really was the queen bee of the tour, the cool big sister. Everyone, including me, looked up to her. That made it all the more painful. The more I tried to ingratiate myself, the more intolerant she seemed.

I did make two friends: Laurel was twenty-three and, like me, more goofy than glamorous. We often went on fun adventures together—once renting bikes and riding over the Golden Gate Bridge into

Sausalito. Holly was only two years older than I was, but way more experienced. She'd take me dancing at eighteen-and-older clubs where I had to lie to get in. I never really talked to either of them about Julie. They both seemed to like me, and I didn't want to tarnish those relationships. They looked up to her, too! I didn't want to give them a reason to ditch me.

Two months into the tour, we went to Houston. Like every other new city, it felt like an opportunity. *Maybe this time I'll walk into the dressing room and feel like I belong. Maybe Julie will smile at me and ask me how my day off was. Maybe the girls will ask me over to their hotel rooms after the show for pizza. Maybe.*

Instead, as I made my way to my seat, I noticed several girls turn their heads away from me as I passed. It felt like an orchestrated diss, like there was a secret pact among everyone to ignore me completely. I finally made it to my chair and felt this crushing realization: I would never fit in. I didn't blame Holly or Laurel for not coming to my rescue—they risked being in the same line of fire. I was in a room with seventeen women and felt utterly alone.

And, really, I was. Even though I called my parents from the hotel lobby, using my prepaid calling card, I never told them what was going on. My mom certainly would not have understood. Mary Anne was still her only friend, and I started to wonder if, like her, I was unable to cultivate friendships. Even worse, the ways in which the girls would ignore me reminded me of my mom's favorite form of torture. Silence. I can't count how many times I would walk into a room and she wouldn't talk to me or even acknowledge that I was there. I never knew what I had done to deserve the silent treatment, but it could last for days. And it always ended with me apologizing or begging her to talk to me—I couldn't stand the silence. With these girls, I decided to wait it out.

I was miserable, but on my weekly phone calls home, I kept things sunny and light. "I found a new dance class that Holly and I are going to check out!" I'd say.

My mom would reply, "Well, that sounds nice! Have fun! Be careful."

The dressing room tension continued for several weeks in Houston, and so I just focused on my job. Being onstage was a relief, because I could at least perform and sing and dance and do things I knew I was good at. The stage was the one place where I felt free.

But then one Saturday evening, during the act 1 finale, "We're Heading for a Wedding," I felt a pang in my stomach. I was dressed in a pink negligee, patting a powder puff up and down my leg as part of the number. I thought it would pass, but instead, I felt another stab in my gut, so strong I stayed doubled over for a moment to regain my composure. I kept singing and dancing, but I suddenly felt light-headed, like I might pass out. I tried to catch someone's eye onstage, wondering if anyone else could tell I was in trouble. Gina Keys saw me looking at her and immediately glanced away. Feeling woozy and panicked, I caught Stacie James's eye. She, too, turned her head from me. I barely made it to the end of the number, where we all wound up on the floor, on our backs, with our legs spread out in second position.

The audience always loved this number, and this night was no different. There was an eruption of laughter and applause, but it sounded very far away. As the curtain fell, I felt as if I was being swallowed by a tunnel. The rest of the cast was getting up and leaving the stage, as we had done countless times, and I tried to do the same. But I couldn't move. I started frantically looking for anyone to notice. I wanted to scream, "Please don't walk away! Please don't ignore me!" But I couldn't. I was paralyzed.

I was still on the stage in my final position when I began to cry. All of the trying to keep it together. All of the trying to rise above it. Stay sweet. Keep smiling. The dam broke. And I began to wail. It was all flowing out of me. The homesickness, the months of not fitting in. The dream job turning into a nightmare. Being ignored. Feeling so alone and so scared. As much as I wanted to run away, I was also desperate for someone to help me, to hold me. To tell me everything was going to be okay.

Thankfully, one of the girls noticed, though I can't remember who.

I vaguely recall the stage manager walking me back to the dressing room.

"What's wrong with her?" someone asked.

By then, my sobs were punctuated with sharp inhales.

"She's just being melodramatic," someone else said.

The next thing I knew, someone was pulling off my negligee and putting me into my jeans and T-shirt, like I was an oversize toddler. I was still in false lashes and streaky makeup when two EMTs arrived and strapped me on a stretcher. As they carried me out the stage door, I remember thinking, *Am I crazy? Am I going crazy?*

At the ER, I cried for another four hours straight. I know now that this was a full-blown panic attack, but at the time, I was discharged with "abdominal pain" as my diagnosis. I don't remember much else about that night other than that the stage manager came to check on me, and that the ER doctor hit on me. When he asked me for my number, I was weirdly flattered! In my flustered state, I gave it to him. After so much meanness, I appreciated what then felt like a kind gesture.

Somehow, I made it back to the corporate housing apartment where I was rooming on my own. Holly checked on me the next day and told me there was an announcement at the theater saying that I was okay and that I just had gas. That was mortifying, but at that point, I just didn't care. Maybe I did just have gas. Maybe I made the whole thing up. Maybe I did just want attention. Maybe I was going crazy.

I ended up taking a week off, and I'm still amazed that I didn't get fired. I'm even more amazed that I didn't quit! How the hell was I going to face that dressing room again?

Meanwhile, the doctor called me, and in my naïveté, I invited him over! I don't know what I was thinking other than he was young and handsome. And frankly, I was thrilled that anyone was giving me any attention. I guess I thought we'd play Scrabble? When he knocked on my door, I nervously let him in and almost had another panic attack when he lay down on my bed! What was I thinking? We didn't kiss, or anything close. I still don't know how I got him out of my apartment—maybe I told him that I was seventeen years old. But how fucked up to be hit on by a doctor while I was having a nervous breakdown! Shame on you, Houston doctor, wherever you may be.

Of course, as luck would have it, someone saw him come into my apartment. My first week back in the show, one of the girls said, "Sutton, you just had this epic episode and now you have men coming to your apartment?"

That was it. I gave up. I stopped saying hello. I stopped engaging. I felt like I was tainted—no matter what I did or didn't do, these girls would never accept me. So I basically stopped talking. I tried to stop caring how they felt, too, which was still hard. But I never missed a show. I kept my head down and focused on my work, and otherwise got really insular. Not surprisingly, the girls didn't even seem to notice. I continued to room by myself. I journaled a lot. And I never told my parents what had happened. When they got the hospital bill, I just said I had bad stomach pains. Later in life, my father told me that they were very close to snatching me off that tour. I think they knew I was struggling, no matter how rosy a picture I tried to paint. I am grateful they didn't try to rescue me.

I turned eighteen that March, and I decided to apply to Carnegie Mellon after visiting the campus when the tour played in Pittsburgh. Holly had started dating Patrick Wilson, who was studying musical theater there and showed us around. Seeing students my age being *teenagers* helped me realize what I was missing. That June, the tour went to Detroit. My parents had moved to Memphis by then, so I stayed in corporate housing with the rest of the cast, but I got to see my high school's production of *West Side Story* and bawled my eyes out sitting in the auditorium. There I was on a national tour, and yet in that moment I felt such regret that I had missed my senior play. I took a Saturday night off to go to prom with a bunch of my high school theater friends, and a Sunday off to walk with my class for graduation, as I had finished those correspondence courses amid the dressing room drama. That weekend was the highlight of that entire year for me.

By the time I left the tour in August, the girls had started being nicer to me. They chipped in to throw me a "happy trails" party. Julie Lamar even gave me towels! Everyone seemed really thrilled for me—or maybe just relieved to see me go. I made it through one year of college, and another half year of living at home with my parents before I wound up back on another national tour—this time with *Grease*. That was thrilling—I knew the movie by heart, and after playing Patty Simcox in middle school, it felt like a triumph to be cast as the understudy to the trifecta of Marty, Rizzo, and Sandy. Three powerhouse roles! I was excited to be back on tour and being paid for what I *love* to do: perform! My brother Hunter was doing *Grease* on Broadway with his girlfriend Jen, so they taught me all the dance moves. That gave me an advantage when I went to the open call, and I was cast on the spot.

I began that tour in San Francisco, at the same theater where I'd started the *Will Rogers* tour two years earlier. But this time, I was determined that it would be different.

So when Mary Ruvolo told me, the very

first week of rehearsals, that Trisha didn't want me to look at her, it was déjà vu. My voice was too big. No one knew how to handle it—not even me at that point in my life. And so, like I had done with *Will Rogers*, I did my job onstage but otherwise turned inward. I didn't even try to get Trisha, or any of the girls on the tour, to like me.

Instead, I started to cross-stitch.

After I finished that Christmas scene for my mother, I decided to make her another piece. I flipped through the pattern book and chose a very colorful design: it was an arrangement of at least twenty baskets of various shapes and sizes. One had a bunny next to it, another was shaped like a heart. It reminded me of something you might see framed at a Cracker Barrel. My mom collected baskets, which she displayed in her kitchen. This pattern reminded me of her.

Whereas the Christmas scene had two colors, this one had at least two dozen: several shades of blue and green, reds, yellows, and peach, as well as warm browns and creamy whites. It was far more complex and less forgiving.

I liked that my new hobby gave me something we could talk about on our weekly calls that reminded me of a happier time in our lives. I would picture her as she used to be, sitting on that living room couch, watching soap operas or *The Carol Burnett Show* while making such beautiful things. She couldn't help me navigate my social circumstances, but she gave me a way to distract myself. Whenever I felt lonely, I had my cross-stitch to keep me company.

One afternoon, I noticed another girl on tour named Laurie working on a cross-stitch project. When I asked her about it, she said, "It's like meditation." We started rooming together and would sit in our double beds watching television while we worked on our various projects.

Six months in, the woman playing Marty left the tour, and I was moved up to play her onstage. I was excited, but talk about more bad casting: she was the most sophisticated of the Pink Ladies, the high school gang who loved to make fun of the more virginal, square Sandy. The other Pink Ladies (Rizzo, Jan, and Frenchie) were all cool girls in real life, too, and had formed their own backstage clique. They were a tight-knit group, and I was the odd girl out. Truthfully, I had no place playing Marty. She was the "sexy" and "experienced" one. Three weeks into the role, I was called in for a meeting with the producers.

"Sutton, we don't think you're right for the role of Marty," one of them said. "We're going to let you go."

I knew I wasn't the best fit for Marty, but I wasn't expecting to be fired. I went back to my hotel room in a daze. Instead of calling my parents or starting to pack, I just picked up that basket scene and sat on my bed. Each stitch was sewn a little tighter that day.

The very next day, the stage manager called: "Sutton. We're in a bind. Trisha is sick, and we need someone to step in to play Sandy. Would you mind doing it?"

I was fired on a Thursday and rehired on a Friday—and was too naïve to question any of it. I just said, "Sure!"

Trisha was supposed to come back the following week, but she never returned. And I continued to play Sandy for six weeks until they asked me to play her full-time. That was another pivotal moment in my career. I could have easily moved home and been done—left the theater world once and for all. Instead, I played Sandy, who was a much better fit for me, on the stage and off. As the lead, I also got my own dressing room, which meant that I could cross-stitch in the quiet. That was even more gratifying than doing it to insulate myself from a crowd.

That basket scene took me an entire year—the duration of my time on the stage as Sandy. It was so intricate! And each stitch got me that much closer to a revelation. I was an extrovert onstage but an introvert in my personal life, much like my mom. I needed this quiet contemplation in order to continue to perform well.

I also saw how each craft I made could be an act of love. In my family, we didn't talk about our emotions. I can remember two times when my mother said the words "I love you" to me. I didn't share the isolation I felt on the road with her, nor did I tell her thank you for pushing me to audition for *Will Rogers* or for inspiring me to cross-stitch. Instead, I made that basket scene for her. I don't remember giving it to her, and I don't know if I consciously thought about my intentions, but I do know that every time I went home when she was still alive, it was hanging in the front hallway, the very first thing you saw when you walked in the door.

DADA'S BLANKET

Like I said before, cross-stitch was my gateway craft. After mastering a few projects, I felt bold enough to try a new medium, and that's what led me to teach myself to crochet. I got addicted right away. People always warn about the dangers of alcohol or drugs in show business, but it turns out the only needle I needed was a crochet hook.

On that tour as Sandy in *Grease*, I strained my vocal cords so badly that an ENT doctor prescribed a two-week vocal rest, during which I was instructed not to speak, let alone sing. I was anxious and scared—I had never lost my voice before. So I moved to my parents' home in Memphis to recover, but I knew that I would go crazy if I didn't find *something* to do. I wanted to try something other than cross-stitch and went to Michaels for inspiration. I thought I might try knitting again, but then I spotted a beginner's book about how to crochet. I was drawn to the simplicity—all I needed was one hook and a ball of yarn.

Back home, I figured out how to make a "foundation chain," the series of stitches that begins any crocheted piece. You start with a slipknot, which you put on your hook. Then you pull the yarn over your hook and through the loop to make a chain. You continue, yarning over and pulling through loops, making as many chains as you'll need for your project. I found the repetitive movements soothing. Losing your voice as a singer is terrifying; crocheting helped me not to dwell on it. Instead of worrying if my voice would ever come back, I focused on that foundation stitch and soon taught myself how to "single crochet," which is the next step after the chain. For that, you insert your hook into a chain, yarn over on your hook, pull up a loop, yarn over again, and pull through both loops on your hook. And repeat.

With each stitch I did, my voice began to heal. With each row I completed, I began to get stronger. And at the end of the two weeks, my voice was back *and* I had made a scarf.

It was incredibly satisfying. Crochet helped me heal, and it soon became a way for me to stay connected to the people in my life I cared about (and those who scared me a bit too).

I decided to make a blanket for Dada while I was on tour with *Annie* as the "Star to Be," a cameo role in the twentieth-anniversary production that was heading to Broadway. This was a big deal! Thrilling! But Dada didn't understand that. He was an old-school Southern grandpa who didn't think that singing and acting was an appropriate career for his granddaughter. My mom, in an attempt to prove to him that unconventional careers were worthy, would send him VHS tapes of Hunter's and my performances. I took it as a hopeful sign when he came to see me in *The Will Rogers*

Follies when we played Charlotte, North Carolina. My optimism faded when, between shows, during a family dinner at the Olive Garden, he turned to me and asked, "Sutton, when do you think you'll be done with all of this theater stuff?"

Still, I sent him letters and postcards from my travels once or twice a month. I wanted to be in his good graces, and to stay connected to him, and to prove him wrong.

Annie was performing in Dallas when I decided to make him a blanket as a Christmas gift. I remember sitting on my couch in the extended-stay corporate housing where the cast was living, eating Christmas M&Ms, listening to *Elvis' Christmas Album*, and crocheting. I used three different colored yarns—dark green, bright green, and red— and a bigger hook to crochet all three colors at the same time for a bulkier blanket. Something he could wrap himself in as he watched his many TVs. (He had four of them all in the same room.) Something that would make him think of me.

After I sent him the blanket, I called to make sure he received it.

"I did," he said in his Southern drawl. "It's very thick."

Dada was a man of few words and, just like his daughter's, they were often cutting.

I knew things were strained between him and my mother. He didn't like that our family lived so far away, and he blamed my father for taking his daughter away from him when they moved to Georgia, while Aunt Mary Anne and her family lived right down the street. When we moved to Michigan, which was like Mars for that side of my small-town Southern family, we saw less and less of them. Things remained strained even when my parents moved back south to Memphis. I was in college when my parents drove to Whiteville for Mary Anne's daughter's wedding. Earlier that year, Mary Anne had won the Pillsbury Bake-Off® Contest with her Fudgy Bonbons, which made the national news. It was a big deal—her recipe was picked from thousands—and it came with a cash prize and a ton of press. There were signs all around town congratulating her, including one on Dada's sprawling front lawn that lit up. He was so proud of Mary

Anne! Her children were getting married! She had won a national baking contest! According to my father, Dada was going on and on about all her accomplishments when he turned to my mother and said, "What have *you* done with your life?"

That cruel comment humiliated my mother.

After that, she stopped sending Dada tapes, stopped calling him. She cut him out. This silent feud lasted until the day he died.

That wasn't the only feud my mom had going at that time—Hunter was also in the crosshairs of her ire. She had begrudgingly used her trust fund from Dada to pay for Hunter's college education. She even made him sign a contract promising to pay her back as soon as he could. Instead, he used the money he made on the national tour of *Cats*, his first job post-college, to buy a one-bedroom apartment on the Upper West Side of Manhattan with Jen, his new girlfriend. (She was Rumpleteazer to his Rum Tum Tugger.) It cost $115,000—a ton of money for two twentysomethings *and* a great deal for a Manhattan apartment! Forget that he was making the smartest real-estate investment ever. My mother was simply furious that he was moving in with Jen—before getting married, and before paying her back! In that order!

Truthfully, my mother had an issue with Jen from the start. Hunter had sent a photo of her home when they began dating in which she was wearing a thong bikini, poolside at the Hard Rock Hotel in Vegas, where *Cats* was playing. After being on tour with dancers for a year, I was unfazed— but my mother thought it was scandalous. "No respectable woman would let her butt cheeks hang out!" she said, aghast.

Meanwhile, Hunter had just been cast as Roger, the "King of the Mooners," in the Broadway production of *Grease*, so his butt cheeks were on a billboard on Broadway! He was breaking all the rules.

My mother sent Hunter books on Christianity and how moving in with a woman before getting married was a sin. She begged him to break up with Jen, and when Hunter refused, she cut him out of her life.

I had just finished my freshman year at Carnegie Mellon and was living at home that summer, which meant I absorbed all of her rage at Hunter. In Detroit, it was aimed at my dad. Next, it was Dada. Now, it was Hunter's turn.

I knew that I could be next and walked on eggshells every day.

In the thick of this turmoil, my college boyfriend broke up with me over the phone. I don't even remember his reason, only that it was very practical, something like "We're young, it's summer, and we're different."

He was my first love, and I just didn't understand what I had done wrong. I was in my dad's bedroom and hung up the phone, crushed. I remember sitting on the floor by my dad's bed, in the dark, when my mom came in and sat next to me, which shocked me. She had been in such a mood about Hunter lately, I didn't know what to expect.

"What's wrong?" she asked in a soft way, which was so unlike her.

I started to cry as I told her what happened. She reached out and held my hand.

It sounds so simple, but it was so rare for my mom to comfort me. We sat in the dark, her holding my hand, me crying.

Not long after, my mom summoned me to the living room.

My dad was there, sitting on the sofa, looking solemn.

"Tell her," my mom said. She sounded upset.

"Sit down, Sutton," my dad said, quietly.

I had no idea what he was about to say—were they worried about me being heartbroken? Was one of them sick? My mind was spinning.

"I had a relationship with a woman I worked with in Georgia," he said, his eyes averted.

My mother was standing near him, arms crossed, trembling with rage.

"When?" I might have asked. My mom was so angry, I thought maybe it was happening now.

"Back when we lived in Augusta," he may have said. I don't remember the exact words, but I do remember being shocked—why were they telling me this now? This perplexed reaction was followed by a wave of relief. It explained so much: the different bedrooms starting in Michigan, my mom's meanness to my dad.

She came into my room later that evening and asked, "How are you doing? Are you upset?" It was like she was fishing for me to choose sides.

"No," I said. "I forgive him."

This made her furious—at him for cheating on her all those years ago, and at me for not being her ally. I was so frustrated! I thought, *If you're going to stay with him, then you have to forgive him.* I had unknowingly absorbed her anger and frustration over this situation for years. It had consumed every part of our family life and had traumatized me. I don't diminish the pain she must have felt, but at that point, we had all been punished enough.

Not long after the incident, I had a conversation with my dad.

"Why don't you just get a divorce?" I asked.

He shook his head and may have mumbled, "It's complicated."

I was so confused why they were still

together because they clearly weren't happy. My father never defended their marriage — but he always stayed put. Out of duty, guilt, and fatherhood. Meanwhile, my mother had managed to cut her father and her son out of her life. My father was holding on by a thread. And I held on too, out of loyalty to him.

That fall, I fell into a deep depression. I decided to not go back to Carnegie Mellon. I had used all my savings to pay for my first year, and I knew better than to ask my mother for a loan. I didn't want to go into debt, and my heart was broken. Plus, I felt like my parents needed me.

I began volunteering at a community kids' theater, started babysitting, and got a job as a singing waitress at the Macaroni Grill, which was like an upscale Olive Garden where the waiters sang Italian arias table-side. While I couldn't open a bottle of wine to save my life, or sing Italian opera, I made up for it by belting hits from *Oklahoma!* and *The Pajama Game*, and made really good tips.

That fall, I gained fifteen pounds from

eating too much fettuccine Alfredo, grilled cheese, and pizza. I cut off all my hair during an unfortunate trip to Fantastic Sams Cut & Color; I looked like D.J. from *Roseanne*. I had stopped exercising entirely and didn't keep up with dancing. I started wearing boxer shorts and baggy clothes. My biggest ambition was trying to collect all of the *Animaniacs* figures in the Happy Meals throughout Memphis. I started to think musical theater might not be the life for me and began to consider going back to school to study science. I was lost—so much so that even my parents were worried. My mother kept asking me what my plans were and at one point tried to set me up on a date with a clown.

I'm not kidding. While living in Memphis, she discovered the casinos in nearby Tunica, Mississippi, and they became her escape. She called them her "happy place," where she could play penny and nickel slot machines while she smoked cigarettes *and* drank all the Pepsi she wanted in a window-less room. My father would drive her to the casinos twice a month. When she returned home after one trip, she suggested that I accompany them next time, because she had found someone for me to date: Zuppo, a clown who worked at the chain casino/ hotel/theme park Circus Circus. That was enough to snap me out of my stupor.

I never went on that date, but I did leave Memphis for Manhattan later that spring. Not because I wanted to—my mother literally circled auditions in the theater magazine *Backstage*, and said, "Go to New York!" This was the opposite of what her father did to her—and I am so grateful. That was just like my mother. She could be infuriating and petty when it came to how she withheld her love and affection to punish us, but she always nurtured my career, and she knew when I needed a little push.

Still, her anger at Hunter reigned supreme: she refused to come see me and my brother perform in *Grease* on Broadway when I was asked to stand in for Sandy for a three-week stint. I was devastated. It was my Broadway debut. But she did come see me as the Star to Be when the twentieth-anniversary revival of *Annie* opened on Broadway. Unlike Dada, she knew what a big deal this was. That was the only opening night she ever came to. Hunter and Jen were there as well, and it was the first time they had seen my parents in three years. My friend Reinaldo, whom I had met during my Memphis days, sat with them, and he said my mother didn't even acknowledge Jen or Hunter. Her resolve was impressive—and so was my brother's. Stubbornness also runs in our family. They both sat there in that audience for two and a half hours, ignoring each other completely.

Around this time, Hunter and Jen got engaged.

When I got the invitation to the wedding, I called home to tell my parents it had arrived in the mail. I was hopeful that this would be the end of the feud. They were finally getting married! My mother confirmed that they got an invite as well, and I was proud of Jen and Hunter for taking the high road.

"Did you RSVP?" I asked, allowing a glimmer of hope to creep into my voice.

"Yes," she said. "I ripped it into pieces and mailed it back."

I felt sick to my stomach.

Throwing the card out would have been bad enough. But tearing it up and sending it in a stamped envelope took thought and energy.

I decided not to let that get in the way of celebrating my brother's happy news. I was so touched that Jen asked me to be a bridesmaid, and even more proud of my father for coming on his own. The wedding was in Rochester, where Jen grew up. During the reception, my dad and I danced, and overall, we had a great time. Jen's family was warm and welcoming. My mother's absence was felt, but it didn't bring anyone down. It was a joyous celebration.

The following week, I called my mother. I wanted to share some of the highlights from the wedding. "Jen was a gorgeous bride," I said. "And Hunter seemed so happy."

Silence.

"Oh, and Dad and I had fun dancing," I said. "He's still got some moves!" I was looking for levity.

"The only reason your father danced with you was to throw it in my face," she said, spitting the words in an angry torrent.

It was crushing. It was also the moment I began to realize that something was seriously wrong with my mother.

My mother's standoff with Dada persisted. And so when I heard he was in the hospital a few years later, I decided to go visit him.

I was on tour with *Les Miz* as Éponine, and we were performing in Washington, DC. Mary Anne called me to say Dada was in the hospital with congestive heart failure. Paw Paw had died of this as well, and both of my grandmothers had strokes. Unhealthy hearts run in my family.

I drove down to North Carolina on my day off to see him. I knew my mother wouldn't go, and in an attempt to do the right thing, I drove down to represent our family.

Dada had always been a larger-than-life man, the definition of a patriarch. To see him in the hospital, attached to all these machines, was startling. He looked so diminished. Even more upsetting was that as soon as I entered the room, he started screaming for his stepdaughter Tammy to come back in. Somehow my presence enraged him. He was literally convulsing, a writhing, angry old man. I thought I was making a peace offering by showing up, knowing my mother wouldn't. But now I think it only made things worse—perhaps because I was her daughter? I don't know.

It was so unsettling that I left the room and didn't go back in. That night I stayed with Mary Anne, and I don't recall her explaining his behavior. But then again, Dada was known to be mean, so it was upsetting but not surprising. I drove back to DC the next day.

Dada died that same summer—and my mother did not attend the funeral.

Mary Anne begged her to come visit and to help out when he was sick. My father told me, much later, that they actually drove to North Carolina more than once to see Dada—but that my mother always panicked once they were there and made him turn the car back around to go home. Was she scared? Ashamed? Angry? I don't know. Mary Anne was hurt and upset that my mother didn't show up, and told her so in a scathing letter. The two sisters ultimately stopped speaking, too.

Soon after he died, Miss Betty, who was Tammy's mom and Dada's second wife, asked if I wanted the blanket I had crocheted him. I said no. I thought maybe Miss Betty would want it as a little piece of the Foster family. I believe it wound up at the Salvation Army.

My last visit with Dada haunted me. Something about me reminded him of my mother at a time when I was beginning to separate from the hold my mother had on me. Why was he so angry at me? Why did my mom refuse to see her father? That stubbornness cost her the only relationship she had beyond my father and me. I was beginning to feel the responsibility of that. She had no one else in her life besides him and me. That was so much pressure!

When I moved to New York, my mother and I communicated mostly by email. One day, not long after she and Mary Anne had their falling out, I opened up a message from her. I stared at the screen trying to understand how I felt about her words: "You are the reason I was born."

AUNT MARY ANNE'S
FUDGY BONBONS

My Aunt Mary Anne won the Pillsbury Bake-Off® Contest in 1994, when the grand prize was $50,000 and a full kitchen remodel! (Fun fact: in 1996, the prize money jumped to $1,000,000.)

Here is her recipe.

INGREDIENTS

- 2 cups semisweet chocolate chips
- ¼ cup margarine or butter
- 1 (14-ounce) can sweetened condensed milk (not evaporated)
- 2 cups all-purpose or unbleached flour
- ½ cup finely chopped nuts
- 1 teaspoon vanilla
- 60 Hershey's Kisses or other milk chocolate candy pieces
- 2-ounce white chocolate baking bar
- 1 teaspoon shortening or vegetable oil

1. Heat oven to 350°F. In a medium saucepan, combine chocolate chips and margarine; cook and stir over very low heat until chips are melted and smooth. (Mixture will be stiff.) Add condensed milk; mix well.

2. Lightly spoon the flour into measuring cup; level off. In large bowl, combine flour, nuts, chocolate mixture, and vanilla; mix well. Shape 1 tablespoon dough (use measuring spoon) around each milk chocolate candy, covering completely. Place 1 inch apart on ungreased cookie sheets.

3. Bake at 350°F for 6 to 8 minutes. DO NOT OVERBAKE. Cookies will be soft and appear shiny but will become firm as they cool. Remove from cookie sheets. Cool 15 minutes or until completely cooled.

4. Meanwhile, in small saucepan, combine the baking bar and shortening; cook and stir over low

heat until melted and smooth.
Drizzle over cooled cookies. Let
stand until set. Store in tightly
covered container.

SHATTERED GIRL

I was a teenager when my mother made a proclamation: "Hunter will be a writer. Sutton will be a visual artist."

I don't remember what inspired her to say such a thing, but I immediately started keeping a journal in order to prove her wrong. Funnily enough, I mainly filled the pages with doodles of interlaced circle designs, as well as drawings of a girl who looked like she was about to take flight. She had big eyes and long, flowy hair, and she was always wearing a floor-length dress so I wouldn't have to draw her feet. In every image, she would be looking off in the distance, often with hands outstretched, reaching toward something.

Even then, I knew that girl was me.

In my midtwenties, I decided to make a painting of that same free-flying girl on wood and then cover her with pieces of glass to create a mosaic effect. I was in LA on tour then, as Éponine in *Les Misérables*, and I asked one of our crew guys for a two-by-three-foot piece of wood to work with. I painted the image first: this girl had long brown hair and was wearing an orange dress, her arms stretched toward a sky teeming with stars in varying shades of yellow.

Next, I went to the hardware store to buy a piece of glass and a mallet. There weren't YouTube tutorials back then so I just winged it. I'm pretty sure I got the idea from an episode of *Trading Spaces* on TLC, my all-time favorite home improvement show. I shattered the glass on my apartment balcony—not the brightest move—and then used a clear epoxy to attach each jagged piece on top of the image, like a jigsaw puzzle. I used a grayish-black grout to fill in the gaps.

I was so proud of the finished result and how the colors were mottled and muted through the prism of the glass.

Each piece of glass represented something. A fragment of who I was, or who I wanted to be. Parts looking for a whole.

On the first day of rehearsals for *The Scarlet Pimpernel*, my fourth Broadway show, another member of the ensemble bounded up to me and declared, "We're going to be friends." We were both dressed in jeans and T-shirts, and neither of us was wearing any makeup. She pointed to my shoes. "As soon as I saw your sneakers, I knew you were my kind of girl." No one had ever approached me in this way.

"I'm Stephanie," she said with a big smile, and I knew she was right about us being friends.

I had never met a more open, outgoing person in my life—certainly not one who liked me! She was also the first adoptee I'd ever met; Stephanie Bast is Korean American and grew up in Bethlehem, Pennsylvania, with an Italian American mother and German American father. She was in a relationship with David, a gregarious guy who had graduated from Yale's super-prestigious acting program. While Stephanie and David were not living together, they were definitely having sex. And I was still very much not. I may have even told her that she was living in sin. She probably laughed at me.

Stephanie was the first friend I could ask *anything*. No subject was taboo. She accepted me for who I was and never judged me (even though I judged her because she was having sex with her boyfriend). We talked about everything—sex and religion, my mother, my brother—and she helped me quickly connect the dots. In my mind, my brother "living in sin," or having sex before marriage, was the reason our mother rejected him. I had subconsciously connected the two, and so my fear of sex was based in the unhealthy fear that the same would happen to me.

Around this time, Hunter was in the Broadway production of *Les Misérables* and told me they were holding an open casting call for an understudy for Éponine. I wanted to play her because she is a fabulously tragic and romantic character. She pines for Marius, then dies tragically in his arms while delivering a note from the woman he loves (not her—*oh, my heart!*). The casting notes say that she is five foot two to five foot four—I've been five foot nine since I was fourteen—but Hunter told me the producers were loosening the rules for the tenth anniversary of the musical. I decided to go to the open call and waited in line at seven in the morning with the other hopefuls.

"What are you going to sing for us?" the casting director asked.

"'On My Own,'" I said. That was Éponine's ballad.

The casting director looked me up and down, glanced at my height on my résumé, and said, "Whenever you're ready."

I got the part.

Once again, I got to share a Broadway stage with my brother. And once again my parents weren't there to see their two children on Broadway. Hunter and I overlapped for three performances before he left to do *Martin Guerre*, a new musical that was premiering in California.

That was a relief, because when I joined *Les Miz*, I had one mission: to have sex.

"The time is now, the day is near," a line from the show's song "One Day More," took on new meaning for me. There were two single guys in the show, but Hunter warned me to stay away from them—I'm not sure why. I immediately made out with one and dated the other, who knew I was a virgin. I am actually so grateful that he was my first sexual encounter, because he was so kind. I wasn't looking for a serious relationship. I was twenty-three and just needed to face my fears. I had started to think something was really wrong with *me*. Maybe I didn't like guys? But I didn't want to sleep with a woman either!

The sex was fast. Nice but fast. After all that buildup, I was like, *Wait a minute, that's it?*

When I was offered to go on tour as Éponine, I said yes. It was a solid job, and I knew I could save money. I was beginning to become fearful of flying—my old anxiety manifesting in new ways. It got so bad that I had to take Xanax before I flew, because I literally thought I was going to die. So rather than taking airplanes with the rest of the cast, I bought a gold Oldsmobile in St. Louis, our first tour stop, and nicknamed her Goldie. I loved the freedom of being able to drive from city to city. Added bonus? I could pack her big, roomy trunk with all kinds of arts and crafts.

I was on the road for about a year, and I made all sort of things: a crocheted blanket for Stephanie, a crocheted backpack for me. I experimented with paper collages, and I painted that flying, floating girl on wood, reaching for the stars, covered with a mosaic of glass. I was so proud of the final result that I took it to work to show my castmates.

"A shattered girl," my friend Aimee Garcia said, admiring the piece.

Her comment spooked me: I had not thought about that until she said it—what was she seeing that I had not?

In January 2000, I decided to leave the tour. I was tired of life on the road and eager to look for my next role. I had also started dating someone in LA and wanted to spend more time with him. So I rented an apartment where I hung this piece. Each shard of glass seemed to represent a piece of me, from that ten-year-old Annie all the way to the five-foot-nine Éponine. I thought I was trying to build a fuller version of myself with each character. But now I saw her in a different way—not in pieces, but broken. I had created a shattered girl.

Art can be a window; it can also be a mirror.

Tom (pseudonym), the man I had started dating, helped me see this more clearly. He seemed so perfect on paper, someone my mother would approve of: he was handsome, Southern, and had inherited a ton of money from his great-grandfather. He was also an aspiring actor with a gorgeous house in Los Angeles and a beach house outside of the city. On our first date, he picked me up in his vintage convertible and took me to Geoffrey's, a really fancy restaurant in Malibu. I was more of a Waffle House gal, and not used to being wined and dined. Bob Saget was sitting at the table next to us. I was impressed! I thought, *I could get used to this!*

For my twenty-fifth birthday, that March, he surprised me with a visit to Vegas and a room at the Bellagio. I was so intoxicated by his wealth and pampering that I tried to dismiss the subtle off-color comments he made, but they got worse with a few drinks and soon were impossible to ignore. He made sexist jokes, and my outrage just egged him on. We got into such a huge fight one night at a restaurant that another couple told us to tone it down. More than once I would end up in the bathroom crying. It was so humiliating. And yet I stayed with him. I have no way to explain this except that it felt familiar.

Meanwhile, Hunter was in Los Angeles finishing *Martin Guerre*. When I was cast in a three-week run of *Dorian* at the Goodspeed Opera House in Connecticut, the two of us decided to drive in tandem back to New York City, where I still had an apartment with my friend Michelle. We'd met on the *Grease* tour and decided to share a one-bedroom apartment on West Forty-Fifth Street as a New York home base.

The night before we left, I packed Goldie for the trip—and placed the wood-and-glass piece on the back seat. The next morning,

I woke up to find the side-panel window smashed and the shattered girl gone.

I was flattered—someone thought it was worth something! I also thought they must have cut the shit out of their hands because I hadn't sealed the edges.

Of all the memories I have with my brother, that four-day road trip stands out. We were in different cars, so I spent the long hours on the road listening to Ayn Rand's *The Fountainhead*. We caught up on one another's lives over diner dinners and breakfasts, comparing stories of life on the road and of our mother, all the while eating at Denny's and staying in Econo Lodges. It was special—a bonding moment. It made me realize how much we had accomplished, considering where, and who, we came from.

As I drove across the country, I kept thinking about that missing glass-mosaic painting. There was something freeing about her being gone—it gave me the space to create a new version of myself.

Months before I left New York on the *Les Miz* tour, I was invited to be in the ensemble for a reading of a new musical called *Thoroughly Modern Millie*. The composer Jeanine Tesori wrote the music, and her then-husband Michael Rafter was the music director. Dick Scanlan, the book writer and lyricist, was good friends with my agent, Steven, who got me the job. This was a musical stage adaptation of the 1967 movie starring Julie Andrews as Millie, a wide-eyed, naïve girl who wants to come to New York City and marry her rich boss. Set in the 1920s, it's fizzy and good-natured, classic musical-theater comedy at its best. I had done readings of new shows in the past, but something about this felt different.

Steven called to say that *Millie* was heading to La Jolla that fall. Jim Carnahan, the casting director, wanted me to audition for Millie! I wanted that part so badly that I flew in from touring with *Les Miz* to audition.

I decided to sing "A Cockeyed Optimist" from *South Pacific*, as the lines from that song, "So they call me a cockeyed optimist, immature and incurably green" summed up Millie—and me too, at that point. That was the first of six auditions.

After the final callback, I reached out to Steven to ask if he had heard anything. I was worried that I had oversold myself.

"You didn't get it," he said.

I was so wound up with anticipation that it was both hugely disappointing and a tiny relief to at least know.

"Who did?" I asked.

"Erin Dilly," he said.

I knew Erin. She had gone to the University of Michigan with Hunter, and we had done a few shows together at the Jewish Community Center in Detroit. She was Peppermint Patty and I was Sally in *Snoopy!!! The Musical*. She was two years older than me, and I looked up to her.

"Do they need an understudy?" I asked. "I really want to be part of the show. I'll do the ensemble."

"Let me ask," he said. Minutes later, he called back. "They do!"

That was such a profound lesson: I didn't let my ego stop me. After doing the reading and meeting Jeanine, Michael Rafter, and Michael Mayer, the director, I knew that I wanted to work with these people. Everyone was so incredibly talented and inspiring. I felt like I could learn from them. That happened in late spring of 2000, and *Millie* was set to start rehearsals in La Jolla that fall.

That summer, Steven called again. "I have exciting news!" he said. "They want you to play Éponine—on Broadway!"

I could hear the buzz in his voice. This was a huge deal—a starring role, on Broadway, where I would make more money than I had ever made before. And yet, I was oddly unmoved.

"I want to do *Millie*," I said.

Steven said, "Let me get this straight. You're turning down the lead role in a hit Broadway show to play an understudy in an unknown play in La Jolla. There is no guarantee that it will go anywhere. *Les Miz* is a surefire thing. Plus, it keeps you in New York."

"I'm sure," I reiterated. "I want to do *Millie*."

I was not interested in being the star of *Les Miz*. I had done that for a year and a half all over the country. I wanted to try something new.

"Call Dick Scanlan," Steven said, exasperated. "Ask him what you'll be doing in the ensemble."

I had gotten to know Dick a little through the audition process. I called him, and he said, "I have no idea what we'll have you do in the show, but all I can say is, trust your gut."

Playing Éponine on Broadway would have been a safe move and an amazing credit to have on my résumé. I knew that I was talented, that I could sing. But I also knew I had so much to learn. I wanted to be in the room with talented people whom I could learn from. My gut was telling me to do *Millie*.

Rehearsals started in September in La Jolla. Erin Dilly was crushing it! She had great timing and made smart choices. I loved watching and learning from her.

A week before we started tech rehearsal, the stage manager called me. "Erin is sick. Can you step in for Millie today?"

I was at Tom's beach house, a two-hour drive away. It was 9:00 a.m., and they wanted me there by 10:00 a.m.

As the understudy, your job is to step in at any time. That means you have to know the role, the blocking, and all the songs, and be able to seamlessly fit in. I zipped down to San Diego, arriving an hour late, and while I had not yet learned all my lines, I knew Millie.

Over the next three days, I crammed and learned the role cold: all the dialogue, choreography, and blocking. That Thursday, we were supposed to do a run-through of the whole show for the creative team. Erin was still sick, so I played Millie. It was amazingly fun—and I nailed it. I was so proud of myself. Then I went back to my apartment to prepare to return to my role in the ensemble the next day.

Friday morning, I was getting ready to go back into rehearsal and was on the phone with Tom when I heard the call-waiting beep. It was Michael Mayer, the director: "Sutton, there's been a change. Erin is leaving the show, and the role of Millie is yours if you want it."

I clicked over to Tom and said, "I have to call you back."

Back on the line with Michael, I tried to make sense of this news: "What happened? Is Erin okay?"

On the one hand I was thrilled! But I was also worried about Erin. And I didn't want anyone to think I was vying for her job— especially her! I was bawling when I went to see her, slightly terrified by the news. She, meanwhile, was serene and kind. Honestly, *she* was trying to console *me*.

There was a tech rehearsal that same day, during which Michael made the announcement to the entire cast. Everyone was in shock. Including me. There was no time to process it. Within hours, I was in a costume fitting. The cast and crew had a choice: they could rebel or support me. I was a twenty-five-year-old freaked-out kid with the opportunity of a lifetime—and they got behind me.

We opened the show in La Jolla, though I have no memory of that first night. We got good reviews and one rave, particularly about me. It was all so overwhelming and thrilling! Meanwhile, Tom was giving me flak about not having any time for him.

Instead of celebrating this moment and supporting me, he was moody and irritable. He was used to me being available most (if not all) of the time, and suddenly, I wasn't. When he complained that I didn't come see him one Monday, my only day off, I was too tired to be stunned. I was singing and dancing eight shows a week, and I needed that time to recuperate. Tom didn't make it easy for me. When they offered me the chance to play *Millie* on Broadway, he was even more threatened.

"So you're moving back to New York?" he said, clearly irritated.

"Um, that's the whole point," I said, annoyed.

This was every theater actor's dream, that an out-of-town show would transfer to Broadway. *Millie* was set to open in the fall of 2001, which meant I had six months free until I had to start rehearsals back in Manhattan. That spring, I accepted a role in *The Three Musketeers*, which was premiering in San Jose, California. Christian Borle was on the cast list, and I was excited to work with him. We'd met at Carnegie Mellon —

he was a junior the year I was there—and I had continued to follow his career. He did the *Footloose* tour with my roommate Michelle, around the same time Hunter was doing the same show on Broadway. He's an oddball, inspired performer and one of our great comedians: Danny Kaye meets Gene Wilder, a true clown. I had a talent crush on him.

I also knew Jim Stanek, who played a lead, because he had gone to Carnegie Mellon, too. They were both such nice guys! We all hung out and had fun together, onstage and off. That helped me realize that I was dating an asshole.

Cut to: Tom coming to visit.

I have this image of him lying on his back in the center of my bed with his hands behind his head, elbows bent, taking up all the space. I realized, at that moment, I was done.

"This isn't working," I said to him right there in the room.

He said, "You're making the biggest mistake of your life."

That was when I knew I had made the right choice.

I trusted my gut by saying yes to *Millie*. And by saying no to Tom. I wasn't sure what was next for me, but I felt I was beginning to assemble all the pieces of who I was becoming. The shattered girl was gone, one of the few art projects I've made that I can't look at.

When I think of her now, she doesn't seem broken to me. I think of her as a girl gathering herself together, ready to take flight.

CRAZY FAMILY DNA

The *Millie* producers were concerned. As the lead of a show, they told me, I was supposed to be "the mayor." It was my job to set the tone for the rest of the cast, and the tone I was setting was somber. One producer even suggested I do a bagel Sunday so that the cast would feel my presence and support.

I was in a hit show and should have felt on top of the world, but I was anxious and unhappy. I began to isolate more and more in my dressing room. To be fair, I was doing it at home as well. Christian and I had been dating for almost a year by then and had already moved in together. My mother knew this but had not cut me out like she had done with Hunter. She just didn't acknowledge that it was happening.

I began to worry. Had I inherited my mother's antisocial genes? Could I handle everything that was happening? All the pressures of leading a company and doing eight shows a week? I felt like I was drowning. I knew I needed to make a change. I needed balance and perspective. The show was all-encompassing. I had nothing left in me to be a good girlfriend, or to even feel like my own person.

I needed help.

Millie previews began on Broadway in March 2002, and right away my mother began emailing me things she had read about me and my performance. She was rarely leaving the house by then. Her main link to the world was the internet, which was how she found message boards and forums on theater-focused websites like Talkin' Broadway and the *Playbill* website. I would receive random notes from her, like

"I read that you cracked on your last note of 'Gimme Gimme' last night," or "Sheilaluvs-bway thought you were great." My curiosity couldn't contain itself—I began to read the boards as well.

That was a mistake. I logged on to one site and did a search for *Millie*—the screen filled with a series of threads with subjects like "Unknown Understudy Takes the Lead," followed by comments about how the producers were taking a giant gamble on me as Millie. We were in the preview period, in which actors get to work out all the kinks onstage before a live audience, leading up to the opening night. Critics don't write about the show until that official date, but that doesn't stop other theatergoers from offering their unsolicited opinions about what they saw. These forums give power to anyone and everyone—one comment emboldens others to pile on. I would sit and stare at the computer, telling myself not to look but unable to help it.

I could feel the pit forming in my stomach and the heat rising in my cheeks as I read things like: "She's a joke." "She's terrible."

"They let her be the star of the show?" "It's embarrassing." "She should go back to the chorus."

And I began to think that it was all true.

There were positive remarks too, which would buoy me, but a negative comment could send me plummeting. It was crazy-making. And it crushed me that my parents, who had not yet seen the show, would start forming their opinions about me based on what strangers thought. I was the lead in a brand-new Broadway musical—I wanted that to be enough. But I also felt the tremendous pressure to prove all the arm-chair critics and naysayers wrong, so I threw every ounce of myself into my performance. I danced and sang harder, and bigger, and louder. I would show everyone that I de-served to be on that stage.

One issue, however, was that I had not yet learned how to sing eight shows a week in order to preserve my voice. By Sunday, it would be trashed. I'd wake up Monday morning, my one day off, and it would hurt to talk. When my voice did crack one night, during "Gimme Gimme," Millie's big showstopping number, I panicked. Michael Rafter suggested I see Joan Lader, a voice teacher and therapist. She is well known in the business for helping singers recover from vocal cord injuries and surgeries, and teaches them to sing in a safe and sustainable way.

During previews, there was a ton of lead-up press—anything to drum up excitement about the production to sell tickets. The producers were pitching the "discovery of a new talent" story *hard*. As a result, in addition to an already rigorous performance schedule, I was doing interviews, photo shoots, and live TV. In the thick of it, I was invited to perform on *The Rosie O'Donnell Show*, which was a big deal. Everyone in the cast and production crew was excited, and I wanted to do my best. It was a Thursday morning, and I had done two shows the day before. When I woke up, I could barely speak. I had been here before, when touring with *Grease*, so I knew my vocal cords were strained. I had flashbacks to when I was put on a two-week vocal rest—this was less than two weeks before opening night.

I got to the *Rosie* set at nine a.m. and told the producer that I was afraid if I did the sound check I might not have anything left for the actual taping. I was paralyzed. I kept thinking, *This is going to be a nightmare! I'm going to embarrass myself on live television.* I knew my parents were watching and anticipated that the message boards would be brimming with "See, I told you so" comments.

I called Joan from my dressing room on set, and she warmed me up over the phone with several trills and vocal exercises. I was still doubtful, but she talked me off the ledge.

"You've got this," she said. "Use your breath. Anchor your body. Your legs are tree trunks. Shoot your roots through the ground. Use your entire body, not just your voice. Your entire body. Your back, your arms, your gut. You have power and reserve within every cell. Use it."

I took her advice and used every ounce of my being to sing "Gimme Gimme." I felt like I barely eked it out, but at the end, Rosie said to the audience, "Can you say, 'Tony Award'?"

I was just so relieved to have pulled it off that I couldn't even let that resonate.

I knew by then that my parents weren't going to make it for opening night. It was originally meant to be in the fall, but then September 11 happened and the entire country came to a standstill. My parents had moved to Florida by then, and my mother's agoraphobia was in full effect; 9/11 gave her a good excuse for being even more terrified of leaving home. She was completely rattled by the experience. The terrorists had learned how to fly planes *in Florida*, both her children lived *in New York City*, and the news was filled with stories of men boarding planes with explosives in their shoes and anthrax being mailed to random people. The outside world became an even scarier place, and my mother used all of these reasons to stay home. Still, I always had this sliver of hope that she would say, "Sutton, nothing would stop us from coming to see you in your big break!" Instead, she seemed exasperated that I would even ask.

When opening night finally came, I found

myself sitting center stage on a black-and-gold-striped pouf about to sing "Gimme Gimme," when the floodgates opened up and I was overcome by all the fears I'd had leading up to that moment. My voice felt strong, and based on the crowd's applause and laughter so far, it seemed like the show was well received. Yet, just before I began to sing, all I could think was: *I want my mommy.*

I made it through the song, and as I flung my arms in the air and hit that last high note, I could hear Christian shouting "Brava!" above the raucous clapping and hollering. I felt the warmth of friends and colleagues who had come to cheer me on—my agent Steven was there, as was Mr. Bodick, my high school drama teacher, who had flown in from Detroit to support me. Hunter would have come, but he was in *Urinetown*, performing down the street that same night. My parents weren't there, but I was still surrounded by love and support.

After the curtain, Christian came backstage, beaming. "I guarantee the reviews will say, 'A star is born!'" he declared.

Everyone felt great about our opening—
after all that hard work, we pulled it off!

And then the reviews came out.

Some papers loved it, but others were
dismissive, including the *New York Times*.
Their lead theater critic, Ben Brantley, was
not a fan, and his opinion mattered. He
didn't single me out, but his dismissive-
ness stung. He had issues with everyone
and everything—including, apparently, my
teeth. Another reviewer wrote something
along the lines of "When she gets to her
second act number 'Gimme Gimme,' all I
could think was, get the hook!" That hurt.

The day after the opening, I stayed in my
apartment with all the blinds closed, sitting
on our blue Jennifer Convertibles couch
alone. That pit in my stomach had grown
bigger than me—I felt like I was being swallowed by it. I thought I had let everyone
down, that the producers made a mistake.
The forums were right: they had gambled
on an "unknown kid," and it had backfired.
Why did they pick me? I was Millie, the girl
on the playbill as well as every NYC bus
and subway poster—and on the marquee of

the Marriot Marquis Theatre, where I had just made a fool of myself. The show was going to close, and it would be all my fault. Going back to perform that night took every ounce of energy I had left. It reminded me of how I felt when I returned to work after my *Will Rogers* panic attack. I had to get up and go do my job, but it was brutal.

In the past, I had turned to cross-stitch, or crochet, or collage to help ease my anxiety—but this time, I started drawing.

Early on in our relationship, Christian had given me a set of colored pencils and a sketchpad. "You're an artist," he said. "You should take your doodles more seriously." Those gifts became my lifeline. Before then, I had never thought that the circular doodles that filled the margins of my notebooks were art. I was touched that he did, and I began to channel that belief onto a blank piece of paper. I started with a black pencil and made small circles on the page. I had no plan. It was all an experiment. I started in the center and the circles began to grow like a web, small swaths of interconnected bubbles emanating from the core, infiltrating the page. I grabbed a blue colored pencil and began to color in a few holes, then switched to a deeper blue, then a lighter one, so these small clusters appeared. Allowing my mind to wander, I grabbed another color at random. Blues became purples, then reds, and the shapes began fingering out from the center of the page in alternating colors of the rainbow, swirling like DNA strands.

When I was finished, Christian framed the drawing and hung it proudly in our apartment. It was the best gift anyone had ever given me.

I was inspired to make another.

My second "real" drawing was of a giant golden sun. I used the same circle style, so that each ray was made up of a cascade of yellows and oranges, small dapples emanating against a rainbow sky.

I was searching for light.

Soon I began sharing my art with Julien Havard, my dresser on *Millie*. That relationship is so intimate—a dresser helps you with the quick changes between scenes, hooking your bra or literally holding up your pantyhose as you slip them on. Julien and I were just getting to know each other—the beginning of a lifelong friendship—and he saw how hard I was working onstage and off. He was an artist and had started sharing his art with me, these beautiful, colorful pop art drawings, often with naughty hidden images of a penis or marijuana joint. I brought my sketchpad and pencils to work one day, and we started drawing together. He used Copic markers, a professional-quality brand of paint pens, and eventually gave me my first set. In between shows, we would sit and sketch on the floor of my dressing room while supping on spaghetti Bolognese from Daniela's. Those calm moments helped me draw a line between Millie and myself. They gave me something to do beyond worrying about what the critics or message boards or my mother thought about me or my performance.

In May, after I had finished a matinee, a producer popped her head into the dressing room and said, "Congratulations! You won the Outer Critics Circle Award!"

I thought I was being punked.

Then I won a Drama Desk Award. Then an Astaire Award. When I was nominated for the Tony Award for best lead actress in a musical, the whiplash felt the most intense. The critics may have been unsure about the show, but the audiences *loved* it. It was a love letter to New York—and after 9/11, it was exactly what people wanted to see: a fizzy, good-natured show about a young girl with a big heart and big dreams. My dressing room was filled with flowers from people like Shirley MacLaine, who sent a card with her bouquet that read, "From one understudy to another," as her story mirrored mine with *The Pajama Game*. Julie Andrews, who played the movie version of Millie, came backstage, too, as did Julie Lamar, who showed up with a scrapbook of clippings that she had saved of me since I left *Will Rogers*. She had been tracking my career and was so proud of me and how far I had come. Every award was a revelation that boosted me, but the Tony nomination was a catapult. When I learned that news, I flashed back to seventeen-year-old me sitting cross-legged in my beanbag chair in Michigan, watching the awards ceremony with my mother. Fast forward a decade, and here I was at twenty-seven, running around to find a dress and shoes to wear to the very awards ceremony that put me on the path to this moment! It was such a rush.

The Tonys are always on a Sunday. The camera run-through for each show that had been nominated for best musical was from 9:00 a.m. to 12:00 p.m. at Radio City Music Hall. The *Millie* cast was performing "Forget About the Boy," so I was dressed in my purple 1920s dress, with my brunette bobbed wig. My brother was there with *Urinetown*, a postapocalyptic musical about corporate greed that had also been nominated for a slew of awards.

We rehearsed our number, went back to the theater for a matinee, then turned around to go back to Radio City Music Hall for the ceremony.

Christian met me at the theater. I have a beautiful photo of the two of us walking down the red carpet—he was just glowing with pride. This was a night both of us had dreamed of, the ultimate celebration of theater and Broadway. We found our seats: fourth row, on the aisle. It was wild! And he was amazing. My cheerleader and champion.

At some point, early on in the evening, a runner came to get me for our performance. Julien was waiting for me backstage to do the quick change. I slipped out of my black strappy gown and into my purple twenties dress as my hairdresser, Darlene, put my hair in pin curls and slipped my brunette bob wig on. Just as I was applying Millie's signature red lipstick, I heard Bernadette Peters introduce the performance: "New York City is always changing," she said. "But one thing remains constant. Young people filled with hunger and hope arrive here every day to make their dreams come true."

It was a complete out-of-body experience. I was trying so hard to be present, but I couldn't keep up with all the feelings: excitement, nerves, terror, giddiness.

Julien said what he still says today before I go out on the stage: "Nice and easy."

The curtain was still drawn as we all assembled onstage. I took my seat behind the row of desks that had been set up, each with an old-fashioned phone on it. Just then, I saw someone run across the stage—it was Gregory Hines!

"Knock 'em dead, girls!" he said with a huge smile.

The curtain rose, the prop phones started ringing, and I launched into the opening line: "No canary in a cage for me!"

"Forget About the Boy" erupted into an exuberant tap dance number where we all burst from our desks and formed two tapping, stomping, and sashaying lines that grew as the whole cast came out to join us for a reprise of the song "Thoroughly Modern Millie." We finished with a final hard tap and outstretched arms. As I stood next to Gavin Creel, the actor who played Millie's love interest, for that final pose, I took it all in. I was on the stage at Radio City Music Hall with many of the same people I had learned lines with in La Jolla a year and a half earlier. The audience burst out in applause, and I started crying. I was so proud! Of this moment, this cast, and this show. It wasn't embraced by all the critics, but it resonated with audiences, and this moment reminded me of that. I cannot tell you how many people have told me they saw *Millie* and wanted to move to New York, do musical theater, become an actor.

Hunter performed after me. He was the lead on "Run, Freedom, Run!," the song the cast of *Urinetown* performed. At the end of it, he pointed at me and I pointed back at him. Two kids from small-town Georgia suddenly performing at the Tonys together, our misfit dreams realized.

A little bit later, one of the runners alerted me that best actress in a musical was next. All I could think was, *I hope my shoes don't trip me up.* The buckles kept catching in the lace hem of my dress. It's so funny how the smallest anxieties can be the focus in such big moments.

Doris Roberts and Jerry Orbach came out on the stage to read the names of the nominees for Best Performance by an Actress in a Leading Role in a Musical. I was up against Nancy Opel and Jennifer Laura Thompson from *Urinetown*, Louise Pitre from *Mamma Mia!*, and Vanessa Williams from *Into the Woods*.

I took a deep breath.

A week earlier, Dick Scanlan, the book writer and lyricist from *Millie*, had come to my dressing room and said, "Do you have a speech prepared?"

I most certainly did not! My Southern humility would never let me be so bold. In fact, when I spoke to my parents the morning of the Tonys, my dad didn't say, "We're so proud of you!" or, "You're a star in our eyes no matter what happens!" He said, "Don't get your hopes up." I know it sounds mean, but I also know they were scared of me getting hurt.

Funnily enough, when I heard my name called, I was oddly calm. The next thing I knew I was walking up the stairs, holding my dress so it wouldn't snag on that darn buckle. Someone handed me an award, I can't even remember who.

I am so grateful that Dick wrote a speech and gave it to me the day before the ceremony—and that I more or less remembered what he had written down, which began, "To say that I am honored is an understatement." It was. I was in disbelief, but my delivery was calm. I wasn't crying or screaming. I thanked the entire cast and the producers and directors for taking a risk on hiring me. I made a point of mentioning Mr. Bodick, who again had flown from Detroit to be there, and Julien. I gave a shout-out to my brother—I could feel him beaming at his baby sister from the audience. And, of course, I thanked Christian, who was so proud. My parents were on that list too. I knew they were at home watching me. I thanked them for all their support for my dreams. That was the real hitch that night, more than the buckle on my shoe. They had so much to do with why I was there, and yet they were not there.

Still, I was floating in giddy disbelief when we went to the Tonys Awards Supper Ball at the Plaza Hotel afterward. Honestly, I don't remember a thing about the party, but I do remember going with Christian to Vintage, our favorite midtown bar, and ordering pizza. We stayed up until four having drinks with all our friends who had been watching the awards from the bar and waiting for us to arrive. We had just moved to a new apartment on Fifty-Fifth Street—which was still empty but for our bed and a couch. That was where I finally looked at my cell phone and saw that I had forty-five voice messages (this was before texting was a thing).

I lay on the empty floor in the dark, still in my Tonys dress, listening to all these voices from my past: Alice Ripley, who played Fantine in *Les Miz*, called to congratulate me. So did Mr. Bodick: "Did you hear me shout when they called your name? I'm so proud of you, Sutton!" There were even messages from old friends from my Memphis days. And one from my mom and dad saying, "Congratulations!" and "Don't drink too much."

I finally felt like one of those girls I liked to draw: floating and free.

I didn't want to go to sleep that night! I didn't want the magic to go away.

My parents finally came to see me in *Millie* that summer. I was so nervous! Even though I had won the Tony, I still felt like

I had to prove something to them. I also knew that being in the city, post-9/11, in a packed theater, made my mother extremely uncomfortable—but she came.

They drove all the way up from Florida and stayed in Atlantic City, so they could spend time at the casinos. They came in on a Saturday morning for the matinee, and I got them a hotel room in the Marriot Marquis so they could order room service instead of having to go to a restaurant. Julien went to meet them in the theater after the show and brought them back to my dressing room. They brought me a Cinnabon and caramel corn that my dad had bought at the Atlantic City boardwalk. They weren't overly effusive—but I think they liked it. Then they left and drove right back home.

I didn't know then that it would be the last time my mother would ever see me on Broadway. They didn't come see my apartment, or ask to see Christian. My mother still refused to acknowledge his existence.

It was around then that the producers confronted me about my unsociable behavior and suggested I host a weekly bagel brunch. By then, I had become friends with Jeanine Tesori, *Millie*'s composer, and I shared with her some of how I was feeling. She gave me the number of her therapist, Joanne, which began a nine-year journey of detangling myself from the web of my mother. I did not yet understand how warped my mom's lens was, or how it distorted my own point of view and experience.

My mother was never officially diagnosed, but Joanne thought she had a character disorder as well as agoraphobia. I looked up character disorders online, and read that they're defined by difficulty behaving in socially acceptable ways, including maintaining healthy relationships with others. That resonated. I also researched agoraphobia. To summarize the Mayo Clinic's definition, it's a type of anxiety disorder in which you're so worried about situations that might make you feel "trapped, helpless, or embarrassed"—and the panic attacks those situations might cause—that you stop engaging with the world in order to avoid them. It's hard to treat agoraphobia, because in order to get better, you have to face your fear. I knew my fear was becoming my mother. What was hers?

I vowed to stop reading reviews and asked Christian to block the message boards on my computer. I begged my parents to do the same, but my mom insisted it was her only way to keep tabs on me and Hunter.

"Mom," I said, exasperated, "why do you want to read horrible things about me and Hunter online?"

"They don't say horrible things about Hunter," she replied.

I kept that sun drawing I'd made hanging in my dressing room, a reminder to seek light, always. And then I wound up hanging the very first drawing I made, the one Christian had framed for me, in my debut art show, a few years later.

I called that piece "Crazy Family DNA."

CHRISTIAN'S MOM'S CHRISTMAS COOKIES

My mother had a set of copper cookie cutters that we used every Christmas to make a plate of frosted reindeer- and angel-shaped treats for Santa. This was one of the sweeter childhood memories I have with my mother. I loved how the kitchen would fill with the smells of vanilla extract and butter, and how my fingers turned a rainbow of colors from the homemade frosting that we used to decorate the cookies after they had cooled. We'd pile them on a plate to put out on Christmas Eve, and I marvel at how I can still feel the magic of these memories every time I pull out those cookie cutters. I'm not sure if they were heirlooms passed down from my great-grandmother or, more likely, something my mother bought from Kmart. Regardless, they are now the cornerstones of my daughter's Christmas, too. That matters most.

I had almost forgotten about making cookies with my mom—until I saw Christian's mom rolling out cookie dough in her Florida kitchen. We had driven down from New York for the holidays, after 9/11 put a pause on the opening of *Millie*. It was my first time meeting them, so to see his mom in the kitchen doing something I did with my own mother moved me. It reminded me of the happier times in my childhood.

"I used to make Christmas cookies with my mom," I said wistfully, hoping she'd invite me to join her.

"Well, you wanna make them with me?" she said.

I felt a flutter in my stomach. "I would love to!" I said.

Christian came into the kitchen, smiling at the two of us making Christmas tree and snowman shapes in the dough before transferring them to the parchment-lined baking sheets.

"What are you two gals up to?" he asked.

"Oh, you know, just making memories," I said.

I loved Christian's parents from the first moment I met them. He and I had been dating six months and were already living together when we decided to do that road trip to Florida. They lived on the west coast of the state, near Sarasota, in a big open house with a huge covered porch called a lanai. Christian warned me that he came from a family of "big huggers," and sure enough, when we pulled into the driveway, they were waiting for us on their front lawn, arms outstretched—literally welcoming me into their home, and family, with open arms. I loved it, and them, immediately.

Beverly Borle had short, sassy brown hair and a raspy cackle. She smoked as much as my mother did, but that was where their similarities ended. Beverly read the *New York Times* and the local Florida newspaper cover to cover and did both crossword puzzles in ink daily. She always had a pair of scissors close by to snip out articles, coupons, and comic strips that she thought Christian would enjoy, which meant we sporadically received big padded envelopes filled with her finds. Christian's dad, Andre, was a retired professor of physiology who spoke with a French/Swiss accent. Like Christian, every time he smiled, he lit up the room. As he was giving me a tour of their house, I took note of all the classy and sometimes suggestive art. One painting was of a nude woman with her legs spread. Christian's dad must have noticed my startled expression, because he said, "What can I say? I'm French!"

Then they showed us to our room. At Christian's house, there wasn't even a question about where I would sleep—with him! Duh! Christian's father and mother were also fabulous cooks, which meant we'd all hang in the kitchen together listening to Blossom Dearie while his father made coq au vin and his mother worked on a tomato tart. I was so moved the first time his parents broke out into an impromptu dance, waltzing around the kitchen. It was so sweet. Suddenly Christian grabbed my hand and we followed suit, dancing with them, buzzed on gin and tonics and laughter.

After dinner, we'd sit on the lanai and play cards. Mr. and Mrs. Borle even taught me how to play bridge. After a few nights, I started to get pretty good. When I tried to ask his father for one more piece of advice, he silenced me and said, "You are no longer a beginner."

I loved them both very much.

Laughter and dancing in the kitchen and fabulous food were foreign concepts to me. I grew up in a household that had liter bottles of Pepsi in the pantry, next to boxes of Krispy Kreme donuts and bags of Doritos. We were a fast-food family, mainly because my mother was a terrible cook. But she was a stay-at-home mom with a husband who traveled for work as a car salesman, so meal preparation fell to her. And she hated it. My mother had bigger dreams than being a stay-at-home mom. Her apathy showed up at the table in the form of soggy fried chicken and pasta with a tomato sauce that I swear was heated-up ketchup with a dash of black pepper. She made boiled cabbage (the worst!) and an underseasoned beef stew so tough it felt like you were chewing on erasers—no taste, but the texture made your teeth hurt. The most international and exotic food we ever had was tacos, from the Ortega kit. The first time I ever heard about coq au vin was in Christian's parents' kitchen.

My dad, on the other hand, loved to cook and would make up for those grim weekday meals on the weekends. Like many Southern men, he takes barbecue seriously. He had a pea-green charcoal grill, and every Saturday evening, he would crack open a Miller Lite and pour lighter fluid over Kingsford charcoal briquettes and newspaper, creating a ginormous fire.

"He's going to burn the house down," my mother would grumble.

The chemical scent of lighter fluid mingling with hoppy beer still reminds me of my dad's cooking—and if I had to pick a last meal, it would be his almost-charred black hockey-puck burgers and the French fries he makes extra delicious by frying a sliced onion in the same pan of oil as the potatoes. My dad, brother, and I would eat these feasts on paper plates tucked into wicker baskets to catch the grease. My mom, meanwhile, would sit with us, picking at an iceberg lettuce salad and sipping her sweetened iced tea.

There was one dish she made that I loved, though. It was a beef Stroganoff that looked like a can of chunky dog food poured onto a plate, but wow, was it delicious! When I left home to go on tour with *Will Rogers*, that was the one recipe I took with me. I made it for years. First you brown ground beef in a skillet, then you add one can of Campbell's Cream of Mushroom soup and a dollop of sour cream. After letting it simmer a bit, you serve it over egg noodles. When Christian and I started dating, I proudly made beef Stroganoff for him all the time, thinking it was fancy cuisine and I was showing off my culinary skills. He loved it (or is a *really* good actor).

By then, my parents had moved to the east coast of Florida, a three-hour drive across the state from Christian's family. I told them that I was driving down to meet Christian's parents, and that I would come see them as well. Neither one of them said,

"Oh, we can't wait to meet him!" They either remained silent or changed the subject, I can't remember which. All I know is that I had planned to see them out of my own sense of duty, and I knew better than to suggest that Christian come with me. It wasn't just to save him from bad food. The last person to come to the house other than me or Hunter was Hunter's girlfriend, Jen, back when my parents lived in Memphis. That visit, meant to introduce his girlfriend to the family, was the beginning of the alienation between Hunter and my mother. I was trying to protect Christian—and myself—from a similar treatment.

We agreed that Christian would drive me halfway across the state to meet my dad at a Krispy Kreme. As we pulled into the parking lot, my dad was already waiting for us, smoking a cigarette and standing beside their cream-colored Cadillac Escalade, dressed in his weekend uniform: jeans and a polo three sizes too big. (For some reason, my dad likes oversize shirts.) Just as he parked the car, Christian looked at me and said, "I'm a little nervous."

I didn't keep any secrets from Christian about my parents—he knew all about their strained relationship with each other, and with Hunter and Jen.

My heart lurched. "Don't be," I assured him. "My dad will be totally nice. Plus, it'll be brief."

He flashed his sweet smile and jumped out of the car.

"Hello, sir," he said, reaching his hand out. I noticed it was trembling.

"Hello, Christian," my dad responded politely, and shook his hand with a nod.

And that was it. I got into my dad's car, and Christian drove back to his parents' house. I thought I was doing this to safeguard our still-fledgling relationship. I see now how his normalcy and openness made my parents' insular dysfunction that much harder to ignore. So the safeguard went two ways: I felt like the only way to continue to have a relationship with my mother was if I just didn't talk about Christian. Even after Hunter and Jen got married, my mother only ever referred to her as "Hunter's spouse." Never by her name. I wish I had fought for her to accept Christian—but I was afraid of being cut off too. With Jen, it was the thong photo. With Christian, it was his bong.

I had been telling my mother about Christian when we were doing *The Three Musketeers*, and she asked me about him as a potential new boyfriend. I must have talked about him a lot in those early days, before we started dating. She had never inquired about my love life, so it caught me off guard, plus I hadn't considered Christian as anything more than a friend at that point. "I could never date him," I said. "He smokes pot." I had seen a bong in his hotel room and assumed it was his. I was still such a goody two-shoes that I looked down on all drugs.

When we did start dating, a few months later, I told my mom we were together, thinking she would be happy for me. She countered, "But I thought he did drugs?"

"He doesn't 'do drugs'!" I said. Truthfully, Christian had stopped smoking even cigarettes (something my mom did until the day she died), but it didn't matter. After witnessing how she perceived Jen, I knew where this was going, and I tried my best to counter her preconceptions, knowing full well how futile that was.

On that visit to Florida, she didn't ask me one question about him or our relationship. When I tried to bring him up in conversation, she cut me off with: "He's not the one. I'll tell you when you've found the one."

Christian was amazingly patient, but I'm sure deep down it hurt. He was so kind, as were his parents. They all helped me realize just how disconnected my parents were from reality—and that I had been held hostage by my mother's point of view. The first major hint of that happened when we first started dating, earlier that summer. While I didn't grow up in a churchgoing family, my mother used Christianity as her moral compass—hence the "living in sin" comments. And I had been doing my own searching, through Bible study classes and attending Sunday services with Michelle, my roommate. Christian and I had only been dating one month when I asked him outright: "Do you believe in God?"

"No," he replied. "I'm an atheist."

I almost fell off my chair—literally. I had never heard anyone even use that term, let alone claim to be it!

"Excuse me?" I said.

"Both my parents are atheists. They raised me as an atheist," he said.

I was shocked and confused. He had all the qualities of a good Christian! He was generous and kind and loyal and ethical— and his name was Christian!

My mother's influence on me was softening. I saw how she used values rooted in Christianity—like saying sex before marriage is sinful—in an attempt to control me and Hunter. But it backfired. Christian helped me find a healthier, happier middle ground.

It was a painful journey, though. We lived together for five years, and every Christmas my parents would send me a holiday card, bank stock, and a box of Florida citrus—all addressed only to me. The first time that happened, I opened the box of two dozen oranges feeling a pang of hope. Then I read the note: "Dear Sutton: Merry Christmas.

Love, Mom and Dad." No mention of Christian. At first, I was embarrassed. Christian just brushed it off—and helped me eat the oranges—but it was such an aggressive diss. I talked to Hunter, who confirmed that all of his holiday cards and gifts were only ever addressed to him. No mention of Jen, either.

Thankfully, I was regularly seeing Joanne, the therapist Jeanine Tesori had recommended. She defogged my glasses and helped me see my mother as a broken woman, which can be so hard when it's your *mom*. She also helped me understand the hold my mom had on me—and my father. Slowly, I began to find my own sense of self, which was like trudging through mud after being programmed for so long by an unhealthy woman. Most poignantly, Joanne helped me mourn the loss of not having the mother I yearned for. I kept wanting and expecting a different reaction. I hoped that she'd come see my opening night in my first starring role! That she would acknowledge my boyfriend's existence! That she would insist on coming to the Tony Awards to support me whether or not I won! I was starting to see that she was incapable of doing these things. I had to accept her for who she was—and stop wanting her to be someone else.

Meanwhile, Christian's parents were always coming to New York for visits and were so supportive. They came to see me perform, which partly made up for the fact that my parents were never there. We would hit the town, seeing plays or sightseeing and going out for fancy dinners. ViceVersa was one of our favorite restaurants. It was on Fifty-First Street, and Christian and his mom would always order the vitello tonnato, which is basically thin slices of veal in a tuna-caper sauce. I thought it sounded disgusting until I tried it, and well…it's delicious! We'd order martinis, eat dessert, have after-dinner drinks, and then stumble home, giddy.

One year, they were in the city on my birthday, and when I came home after a matinee, they surprised me with a Pink Cake from Amy's Bread, my favorite. My parents always acknowledged my birthday, usually by sending a card, but they were never physically there. Christian's parents showed up in all the ways my parents could not.

When we got engaged, we sent his parents a photo of us together, me proudly wearing the beautiful square-diamond vintage ring he gave me, as our announcement. They called us as soon as they opened it, and put the phone on speaker so they could both congratulate us together. "Welcome to the family!" his mom was shouting into the receiver joyfully, his dad laughing.

Buoyed by their reaction, we called my parents. We hadn't sent them a photo, but I was excited to tell them that we would no longer be "living in sin"!

My mother answered.

"Mom, I have some exciting news. I'm engaged!" I said, then waited for some response.

Silence.

I heard her pass the phone to my dad.

"It's Sutton," she said.

My heart deflated as I told my dad my news. Christian couldn't hear the conversation, but he was by my side. His smile faded with mine.

"Okay," my dad said, sounding subdued.

I hung up and tried to remember Joanne's advice, but it was hard.

I decided to shift the narrative: no more protecting anyone. Now that we were engaged, it was time for Christian to get to know both of my parents, the people who raised me—and that meant more than a handshake in a parking lot. Enough was enough. I knew they weren't going to come to New York to meet him, so I had to bring him to them. My hope was that once my mother met him in person, she would see how much we loved each other and would support our marriage. That he wasn't some drugged-out druggy drug dealer, or whatever image she had created in her mind. That maybe she would even help me pick out my wedding dress and that she would come see her daughter get married. Christian knew the story of Hunter's torn-up wedding invitation. Still, he was game to meet them. He knew how important it was to me.

This was 2006. Christian was in *Spamalot* at the time, and I was in rehearsals for the Broadway run of *The Drowsy Chaperone*. We flew down to Florida after his Sunday matinee and drove straight to my parents' house. We stayed at a hotel in Orlando and planned to go to Disney World the next day as a palate cleanser after what I knew would be an emotionally exhausting experience, whether it went well or not.

Christian was the first visitor besides me who had ever entered their Florida house. It was a block from the beach and reeked of cigarette smoke. They had bought new furniture when they moved from New Jersey — their sixth move in my lifetime — so nothing was familiar to me other than the cross-stitch basket scene I'd made for my mother, which hung in the entryway, and an afghan blanket that lay at the foot of her bed. They were the two constants throughout all those moves. Her room was downstairs, my dad's upstairs. I had explained all this to Christian, so he wasn't surprised by any of it. He was such a trooper. That evening, my dad got Sonny's BBQ and sat with me and

Christian at the kitchen table. My mom was perched on a barstool—at the table, elevated, not on the same plane. She didn't even fix herself a plate. I can't remember what we talked about—only that we ate quickly and then said our goodbyes.

"It was nice to meet you," my mother said. She was cordial, but there were no hugs, handshakes, or laughter. And certainly, there was no dancing in the kitchen—not that I was expecting it. Still, I had hoped Christian's charm and kindness would thaw her toward him, and us. I say "her" because I was never worried about how my dad might react. If anything, he just seemed numb. I honestly couldn't understand why he stayed with her all those years. But then again, I kept coming back, hoping this time she might change. Maybe he kept hoping she would change, too. On that trip, I kept looking for a flicker in her, but she was unmoved, so stubborn.

She did suggest that Christian and I take a walk on the beach after dinner, which was a relief—I couldn't wait to leave. I didn't know yet that she had never visited that beach, even though she was the one who insisted they live near it. Christian and I walked hand in hand toward the ocean, breathing in the salty air. It felt cleansing after being in the stuffy, cigarette-scented house. We kicked off our shoes and dug our toes into the sand and looked up at the full moon bright in the sky.

"I'm so sorry," I finally said.

Sorry that I didn't have a normal family. Sorry that they didn't embrace him like his family embraced me. Sorry that it was so complicated.

He just hugged me tight. And then we drove back to our hotel in Orlando and drank Manhattans at the bar.

Christian and I decided to get married at the Brooklyn Botanic Garden—I wanted to be barefoot with flowers in my hair at an outdoor ceremony. I called home to tell my parents, once again excited to share my vision with them.

My mother's response stunned me into silence:"You knew if you got married in New York I wouldn't come."

How does one respond to that? That was her power—her way of controlling things. I was beginning to piece all of these things together in therapy.

"If your mother were physically disabled and couldn't move, would you ask her to walk?" my therapist asked.

"Of course not," I said.

"You have to think of your mother's agoraphobia that way. She is emotionally unable to be in the world. She is unable to leave her own home. She cannot do it. No matter how many times you ask. You must accept that. And stop expecting a different outcome."

I was beginning to understand this, but it was still crushing.

While I knew she wasn't able to come to my wedding, I still wanted her to be there. Just like I wanted her to be at my opening night of *Millie*. I always made excuses for why she wasn't there—she hated the crowds, 9/11 intensified her fears—and gave her a way to excuse them. But it did not take away from the feeling that I wanted my mommy to be at my wedding. The mantra "acceptance without expectations" helped me make sense of her meanness— but it didn't always lessen the pain.

Christian and I planned and paid for our wedding together. I handmade every single save-the-date card and our wedding invitation, too. I had a crafting night instead of a bridal shower, which Julien hosted at his art studio on Avenue B. My friends Stephanie and Michelle came, as did Megan McGinnis, a new friend I had met on *Little Women*, which I did right after *Millie*. Hunter and Jen joined with a few other friends, and we drank champagne punch and made cake toppers out of Sculpey clay, which is like Play-Doh for grown-ups. We picked our favorites, a simple bride and groom made by our good friend Joe Farrell and his girlfriend Jen Taylor. It went on top of an extra-large Pink Cake from Amy's Bread.

We got married on September 18, 2006, on a beautiful grassy lawn near the glass greenhouse at the Brooklyn Botanic Garden. One hundred fifty people came, including my dad and both my aunts—Mary Anne and Linda, my dad's sister. Christian's parents were over the moon—his mom was buzzing around among the guests, so incredibly proud and excited. Stephanie and Megan sang "My Romance" with Joe Farrell and Jeff Dattilo as my dad walked me not down the aisle but into a circle that everyone had formed holding hands.

"Dad, thank you for being here," I said as I linked my arm through his. "It means the world to me."

"I'm not missing my daughter's wedding, no matter what wrath I might face when I get home," he said as he kissed me on the cheek. "I wish your mom could see how beautiful you look."

"I love you, Daddy," I said.

I wore a gauzy Vera Wang empire-waist dress and a flower wreath in my hair. Michael Rafter conducted, and we all sang "Till There Was You" from *The Music Man* with Patrick Wilson and Matt Stocke on ukulele.

Christian and I were married beneath a willow tree.

And my mom, true to her word, was not there.

After we got married, I asked Christian's mom to send me a few of her favorite recipes. I wasn't naturally a good cook, but I wanted to learn. I had visions of Christian and me cooking and dancing in the kitchen as we prepared delicious meals, just like his parents. She sent me envelopes of printed-out and handwritten recipes: that coq au vin, her famed tomato tart, a pasta carbonara, and chicken cordon bleu. I also asked her to share her Christmas cookie recipe with me, which she dictated over the phone. I wrote it in pencil in a yellow Mead notebook, which now lives in my kitchen.

I started making those cookies every year for Christmas—and continued, even after Christian and I separated. After my mother died, when I helped my father clear out the Florida house, I asked him if I could have her copper cookie cutters and all the cross-stitched ornaments—the happier heirlooms, the ones I want to pass on to Emily.

Now, I make Mama Borle's Christmas cookies with my daughter. Both of Christian's parents have also passed away, but that recipe lives on. We pull out those cookie cutters, and Emily climbs up on her periwinkle-blue stool and helps me add all the ingredients into a big ceramic bowl, flour dusting our clothes and noses as we measure and stir. We then roll out the sticky dough and make shapes of Christmas trees, and angels, and reindeer, sneaking tastes of raw dough and waiting patiently for the cookies to cool so we can ice them, licking our rainbow-colored fingers and laughing.

My mom never got to meet Emily, but in a way, Emily gets to know her grandma through this sweet ritual, one I have made my own for my daughter, borrowing from Christian's mom's cookie recipe and infusing the experience with her big heart. I even use homemade vanilla extract made by Marilyn, my dad's lady friend whom he met after my mom died. For me, it was a lesson in how you can pick and choose different life ingredients, focusing on the sweetest ones, mixing them all together.

Recently, my husband, Ted, smiled as he walked into the kitchen.

"What are you two gals up to?" he asked.

"Oh, you know. Just making memories."

MAMA BORLE'S
CHRISTMAS COOKIES

Ingredients

- 1 cup (2 sticks) butter, softened
- 1 teaspoon vanilla extract
- 1½ cups sugar
- 3 eggs
- 3½ cups flour
- 2 teaspoons cream of tartar
- 1 teaspoon baking soda
- ½ teaspoon salt

1. Preheat the oven to 375°F. Cream the butter and vanilla together, then add the sugar gradually until the mixture is light and fluffy. Add the eggs one at a time with an egg beater.

2. Separately sift the dry ingredients and gradually fold them all into the wet ingredients with a spatula. Refrigerate for three or four hours, until cold.

3. Using a rolling pin, roll out the dough on a floured surface until it's ⅛ to ¼ inch thick. Cut the cookie shapes out using your desired cookie cutters and place them on an ungreased cookie sheet.
4. Cook at 375°F for 6 to 8 minutes. Cool on a rack before icing.

ICING INGREDIENTS

- 1 stick unsalted butter (soft)
- 4 cups confectioners' sugar
- ¼ cup milk
- Add drops of food coloring to desired shade (optional)

1. In a large bowl or stand mixer, beat together the butter, 2 cups of the confectioners' sugar, the milk, and the food coloring (if desired).
2. Add the remaining 2 cups of confectioners' sugar and beat until smooth. Use to decorate cooled cookies.

MAMA HELEN'S BEEF STROGANOFF

Ingredients

- 1 (12-ounce) package egg noodles
- 1 pound ground beef
- ½ yellow onion, diced
- 1 (14-ounce) can cream of mushroom soup
- 1 dollop sour cream (or to taste)

1. Cook the egg noodles according to the package instructions.
2. In a large skillet, over medium-high heat, cook the ground beef with the onion, stirring occasionally, for 6 to 8 minutes, until browned. Once it's cooked, drain the excess fat.
3. Add the cream of mushroom soup in the same skillet and stir to combine. Stir in the sour cream.
4. Serve over the cooked egg noodles.

FAILED PROJECTS

For every project that I have worked on, mistakes are an integral part of the process. Sometimes I embrace them and include them in the final piece—little reminders that life isn't perfect, and there is beauty in the imperfections. With each mistake, you hopefully learn something you can bring to the next project you work on.

But some things are beyond repair and not worth fixing. I have learned that you just need to let those go.

1. Precious Moments

During the *Grease* tour, I decided to make a wedding gift for my fellow cross-stitching pal

Laurie. I chose a sweet image from a Precious Moments pattern book of a bride and groom riding in their honeymoon car, streamers and flowers and cans flowing behind them. I worked on the pattern for months, but at one point I took a break and stashed it away in a tote bag with the linen still taut in the embroidery hoop. When I finally picked it back up, I noticed that the hoop had left a stain. A faint light-brown circle was now in the center of the project, intersecting the getaway car and slashing across the bride's face. I was mortified. But instead of handwashing the project, I just had it framed with that damn ring stain. I gave it to Laurie and hoped she wouldn't notice, but it was pretty hard to miss.

My advice?

Stains happen.

Wash them off before framing! Once it's framed, you're screwed.

2. CHEESY MUFFINS

The Scarlet Pimpernel played the Minskoff Theatre, which is on Broadway between Forty-Fourth and Forty-Fifth Street. The year I was in the musical, the company was invited to watch the Macy's Thanksgiving Day Parade from the third-floor lobby, which overlooked the route. It was thrilling to see the gigantic floats bobbing above the crowds and the Rockettes high-kicking their way down the avenue. Bonus: we didn't have to stand outside in the cold.

Inspired, I decided to bake some muffins to share with my cast. I am not naturally a good cook, but I love to bake. I chose a cheese muffin recipe, but I didn't have enough butter, so I used olive oil as a replacement. I proudly offered them to my castmates and watched as each, one by one, took a bite and then spit it right out.

My advice?

Taste what you make before you share your food with friends.

And be careful with substitutions.

3. A Crocheted Cardigan

During the run of *The Drowsy Chaperone*, I decided to crochet myself a cardigan. It was my first attempt at making clothes. I chose a burnt-orange-colored yarn and a pattern from *Crochet Today!*, my favorite magazine.

(Some gals dream of being on the cover of *Vogue*, but my bucket list was being in the pages of this publication, which I subscribed to until it stopped printing.) I crocheted the back of the sweater first and was so excited that I didn't take the time to check my gauge, which is basically how many stitches you make per inch; I have a tendency to do a tight stitch. I jumped right ahead into making the sleeves, again without checking any measurements. I worked on that sweater for a solid week, and by the time I finally tried it on, the sleeves weren't wide enough to cover my arms and the sweater was so snug that it wouldn't connect in the center. That sweater was abandoned and shoved in a bag, never to be worn.

My advice?

Always measure your work.

If you're making clothes, take the time to try the clothes on as you go, ensuring that your work will fit.

And always, always check your gauge.

4. Hope Collage

While I was doing *Young Frankenstein* on Broadway, I decided to make a collage. I printed out the word *hope* on printer paper using all sorts of different fonts. I must have had over five hundred little pieces of paper with the word *hope* on them. I used Mod Podge and decoupaged them to a 24-by-24-inch canvas, starting in one corner and emanating out so that they overlapped each other and together looked like a volcanic eruption of tiny words. I brushed black and red paint to fill in the edges of the canvas.

As I looked at the final product, it still didn't feel complete.

One night, I had an idea. I took the canvas to my sink and set it on fire—the idea was to create a cool visual effect. I burned blistering holes into the center and watched as the words began to catch flame.

Instead of completing the piece, I ruined it.

My advice?

Don't set your work on fire, unless you are ready to let it go.

5. My First Marriage

DIVORCE BLANKET

I was on the corner of Forty-Second and Eighth Avenue, in front of the Auntie Anne's pretzel place, when my agent, Steven, called.

"Have you heard?" he asked.

"Heard what?"

"There's a mention in Page Six about you and Christian."

It was a drizzly day, and this news stopped me midstride. I looked down, and at that very moment, saw the *New York Post* open to the page with my photo on it, lying in a dirty puddle. (You can't make this stuff up.) The headline was something like: "Sutton Foster's Roll in the Hay Is Going to Ruin Her Marriage."

There was no need for me to look any closer. I knew exactly what it was referring to.

"Roll in the Hay" was one of my numbers in *Young Frankenstein,* the Mel Brooks musical I was doing on Broadway. I played Inga, the sexy German fräulein that Teri Garr originated in the movie. The titillating tabloid story insinuated that I had cheated on Christian—and pinned our failed marriage on me. I felt like my purse had been dumped on the sidewalk.

As I headed into a rehearsal for *Shrek the Musical*—the next musical I was joining once I finished my *Young Frankenstein* commitment—my mind was racing.

Christian and I had been separated for six months and were both dating other people. This was a very painful agreement we had made, as shortly after we got married, we realized that we both wanted more from our relationship. We were best friends and frankly more like roommates than partners.

The gossips tried to sum up our demise as simply and salaciously as they could, but it wasn't that clear-cut. The only two people who really know what happened are Christian and me. And I'm going to keep it that way. I will say that Christian and I were brutally honest with each other the entire time. There were no secrets. No one cheated. Our separation was actually fueled by love for each other. But that type of story doesn't make for a good headline.

To make matters worse, my mother, who read everything online, called me, seething: "How could you do such a thing?"

It was shocking to me that someone who seemed to care so little about Christian while I was with him suddenly took such a rabid interest in his well-being.

"You don't know what you're talking about!" I fired back, furious.

I had already told my mother that Christian and I had separated, but she was reading and believing all the message board gossip that the story generated. I had to spend the next hour defending myself, in my most vulnerable moment, to my mother, who had never accepted Christian in the first place. That was crushing. After I hung up with her, I again felt this all-consuming emptiness. But this time, there was no Christian to pull out the sofa bed and order pizza. That realization sent me spiraling.

All I wanted to do was run away. Leave New York. Get the hell out of there! But I was still playing Inga and had to figure out how to quiet the cacophony in my brain. I decided to pick up my crochet hook again.

This time, I wanted to make a granny-square blanket similar to the one my mother had kept at the foot of her bed for as long as I can remember. It looked like something you might find at a garage sale: a classic seventies olive-green-and-brown afghan throw that smelled of cigarette smoke and was neither soft nor cozy. It reminded me of my mother—and was the one thing I identified with the idea of home. It was the base for my handstand and front walkover practice when I was a kid in Augusta, when my parents still shared a bedroom, and it moved with my mother to her room when they started sleeping in separate quarters in Michigan. It came to Memphis, and the last time I spotted it was at the foot of her bed in Cape Canaveral.

I'm still not sure why I was so compelled to make my own version of that blanket at that point in my life other than because I felt untethered. I couldn't control what people said about me and Christian, whether in the tabloids or even in the theaters where we both worked. But I could choose the colors that went into each granny square, and I could choose the pattern I wanted to make. I found one with a beautiful flower design. Onstage, I had to sing and speak with a thick German accent, wear a corset, and yodel. Backstage in my dressing room, I was obsessively crocheting 4-by-4-inch granny squares, each with a flower blooming from its center.

The first square was like solving a puzzle. You begin in the center, making a magic ring, which is basically a loop that can expand and contract. You crochet your first stitches into that ring and continue working in a circle. As I finished the first flower, an intricate design of petals three layers deep in a beautiful hot-pink wool yarn, I wondered...how did our marriage dissolve so fast? What went wrong?

I thought we had followed the right pattern. Our lives were so deeply intertwined: we shared friends, our dog Linus, and even the stage in *Millie* when Christian replaced Gavin Creel as my love interest, which meant we both worked *and* lived together. And we did it well.

I grabbed a light-pink yarn of the same scratchy wool and began to crochet into the flower to build the background, each stitch helping me begin to untangle what possibly went wrong. And yet, there were no early warning signs. No major red flags. No big fights. As the pink border began to grow, I noticed that my finger was also growing red; I had wound the yarn too tightly around it, working it with my hook, making tight loops as I went.

Christian and I were best friends, who had created a good life together—and we both realized we needed more than either one of us could give. But neither of us could define what that was. All these thoughts tumbled through my head as I grabbed my scissors and snipped the pale-pink yarn off, disconnecting it from the ball. I added an

olive-green wool to the edge of the background and began to make the border.

We tried couples' therapy. I wanted to
fight for our marriage, but Christian had
already fallen for someone else. When I
watched him take off his wedding ring in
one session, I knew it was really over.

I held the finished square in my hands.
This hot-pink flower, rimmed with a dull
green. A promise of something blooming.
It gave me a small burst of hope, possibility,
even though the ground around it seemed
infertile. Dead.

Christian moved out of our apartment
and got a place about a block away. And yet
for months, I kept unscrewing my brush tip
from the electric toothbrush we had once
shared, as I had done every morning and
night for five years, before realizing that it
was no longer necessary.

I also began focusing more on my friends.
I realized so many of my friendships had
taken a back seat to Christian and his
friends. (I'm a Pisces, which means I am
a great absorber of people—great on the
stage, but tough in relationships.) When he

moved out, there was this big void I needed to fill. My friend Megan would come over to watch a movie and then wind up sleeping over, or my friend Kevin Covert would just show up with a bottle of white wine and we'd watch *America's Next Top Model.* Stephanie had moved to LA, but we spoke on the phone almost every day. Through the pain of the breakup, real and lasting relationships were forming.

And all the while, I was obsessively crocheting—and also eating too much chicken salad, which I'd pick up on my way to work from a health-food joint called Green Symphony. When my corset started to dig into my belly, I asked Julien, "Did they dry clean my costume?"

"Um…probably?" he'd lie, as he grunted while attempting to pull the corset tighter and tighter.

I'd suck in my gut as much as I could— often while crocheting at the same time— and soon started standing because the corset dug into my stomach if I tried to sit down.

"What are you going to make with all of

those squares?" Julien asked one day, while watching me stand in the doorway crocheting away.

I had a stack of at least twenty beautiful squares. Each one with a perfect flower, in varying jewel-tone colors.

"I don't know," I said. "I'm just making them."

It felt like I was pouring all of my heartache into each and every stitch. All of my regret and shame and mistakes and fear. All of it was going into each square. The life I had been building for the last five years had completely unraveled.

I made stacks and stacks of squares. And that became a visual reminder that I *was* making progress. That even though my heart was broken, I was still moving forward. Each time I placed a finished square on one of the piles, it reminded me that I was healing. My garden was growing. Even if it didn't feel that way on the inside.

Slowly but surely, those crochet piles multiplied.

After nine months playing a sexy fräulein, I was slated to play Princess Fiona in Broadway-bound *Shrek*. By then, I had made close to one hundred squares. I still didn't know what to do with them—I had more than enough to make one gigantic blanket, or two twin bed covers, but I wasn't ready to stitch them all together. I didn't know what their purpose was. Not yet.

As I was packing up my dressing room, getting ready to go on the road with *Shrek*, I simply shoved them all in a black Hefty garbage bag and stored them in my closet. Or rather, Christian's old closet, which I had turned into my craft storage.

I would figure out what to do with them one day.

I played Fiona, the burping and farting ogre princess in *Shrek*, for a year—and crocheted seven blankets. When the musical closed in January 2010, I was ready for something totally different.

Joe Machota, an agent who was courting me, suggested me for the role of a dominatrix in a play called *Trust*, by Paul Weitz. I had never done a play, only musicals, and I was looking for a challenge. Going from

Millie to Fiona to a woman who dressed in a pleather corset and walked around onstage cracking a whip was intriguing to me. It was exactly the type of left turn I wanted to make in my career. It was sexy and a bit dangerous, and those were things I felt might be exciting to explore both onstage and on a personal level.

The play was all about role-playing. My trademark had been spunky, people-pleasing Southern charm: "Don't forget to smile! Yes, ma'am! No, ma'am!" I had always been able to hide behind my tap dancing, high notes, and humor. *Trust* forced me to survive on a stage without song, and with my own sexuality in the forefront.

My audition was with Zach Braff. I knew him from watching *Scrubs* though I had never met him before. For the audition, I'd have to crawl on top of Zach. It was a very sexy scene, and I asked Megan to help me prepare. I made her sit on my bed and did the whole scene with her first, thinking, *If I can seduce Megan, I can seduce anyone.* I even went around dominating poor Linus the dog.

Trust was how I met Bobby Cannavale. He was also in the play, and in real life, he was a dark, brooding, gorgeous, but also goofy movie star. Earlier that year, I'd bought a lake house an hour outside the city, close to where my brother and Jen also had a weekend home. That felt like another bold move: I had saved enough money to buy a house. So I did.

I invited the play's cast up to the lake house for a night. The four of us—me, Zach, Bobby, and Ari Graynor—all drank wine around a bonfire. That was when my romance with Bobby started: we shared glances over the flames, and he lingered at my bedroom door before heading to bed.

A week later, we started dating. He invited himself to my lake house. I said yes. He was the perfect combo for me at that moment in my life: it was summer, I was single, and I had a role in this weirdly sexy play. It was super flirty and fun and unlike anything I had ever experienced before. He drove me crazy in the best way. I felt like a teenager, giddy and excited. We'd meet in the after-noons before our shows, and it was a mix of romantic and hot and something that I had been missing. I craved him. We fell in love and couldn't get enough of each other.

On the Fourth of July, I invited him up to the lake for a boat trip with Hunter and Jen and some of their friends. I have this photo of Bobby and me napping on the boat, our bodies intertwined. So in love and happy.

That fall, I was offered the part of Reno Sweeney in *Anything Goes*. As he had done with *Trust*, Joe Machota planted a seed with Kathleen Marshall, the director and choreographer, that I could be a Reno who sings *and* dances. Ethel Merman originated the role, and Patti LuPone did a revival in 1987. Both of their Renos sang while the ensemble danced. In this production, I was going to get to do both. I was flattered. And so naïve. I didn't know it yet, but I was leaping into the pool and had no idea how to swim.

Bobby and I went to visit his family in Miami over Christmas. We drove down in his new red Prius, with his fourteen-year-old son, Jake, in the back seat, while I crocheted a Christmas tree garland in the front. His mom and sister and brother were super warm and welcoming. We left Jake with them when we went to see my parents.

I didn't want to make the same mistake I'd made with Christian. I was in love with Bobby, and I wanted my mom and dad to meet him right away. So Bobby drove us the three and a half hours from Miami to Cape Canaveral. I was nervous—but this time it was different. Bobby was movie-star famous, and my mother was smitten. When I first told her Bobby and I were dating, she was excited. That was new to me. She knew nothing about him beyond the films he had been in and the stories she had read online.

We walked into the house, which of course reeked of cigarette smoke. Maggie and Mitzi, my parents' two shih tzus, went bazonkers— they weren't used to having people in the house. Neither were my parents. We all just stood awkwardly in the entryway while my parents paced around us, unable to settle.

"Can we please just all sit down?" I finally said.

We did, about five feet from the front door

on the entryway bench and some chairs. My dad had made chocolate chip cookies, which he served. He and my mom were so nervous and awkward—it broke my heart. They were trying so hard. *"The Station Agent* is one of my favorite movies," my mom said, trying to make conversation. We talked about our visit to Miami and a little bit about *Trust*. It was *pleasant*. We were there for about forty-five minutes, and I knew that was enough. I hugged them both goodbye, and then my mother shook Bobby's hand and said, "It was very nice to meet you."

She was smiling.

Back in the car, I burst into tears.

After the tension between Christian and my parents, I had been bracing myself for a similarly awkward experience. Bobby didn't understand why I was crying. He had heard most of the stories about my parents, but he couldn't really understand that what had just happened felt normal in a way that was visceral and painful for me.

Bobby and I decided to go to London to celebrate the New Year. His son Jake had just turned fourteen, and Bobby told me on that trip that he didn't want any more children. He was adamant about it. I was thirty-five, and I was surprised at how upset I got. I had never been front-footed about having children—and had not even considered having them with Bobby yet. But I at least wanted to have the conversation! That night, I wound up crying in the bathroom. I stared at my face in the mirror. Tears streaked down my cheeks. I was so confused by my reaction.

Did I want children?

Rehearsals for *Anything Goes* started that January, and Bobby began rehearsals for a new Broadway play, *The Motherfucker with the Hat*. We were going to be on Broadway at the same time! We went to each other's opening night parties. And then we both got nominated for Tony Awards. It was an unbelievably exciting time, and we were doing it together.

But Bobby was starting to pull away. I could feel it. Our hot and sexy romance was beginning to fizzle. Gone were the afternoon romps and stolen glances. I so badly wanted us to be perfect for each other that I had even started thinking that we were going to move in together.

That June, Bobby had to have shoulder surgery, the result of an injury he had sustained during a fight scene in *Motherfucker*. His accident happened onstage on my opening night, and he showed up to that party in pain. It was the biggest night of my career— the critics loved the show—and I spent it worried about him instead of being able to celebrate being in a huge hit Broadway musical. That summer, as he was healing, I signed up to be his nurse. I took him home from the hospital, shopped for food, picked up his medicine, and did my best to take care of him, which left no time to take care of myself or even ask, "What do I need?" I was still in therapy, and I remember my therapist being concerned: "Who is taking care of you?" she asked. My hairdresser said something similar: "I hope this is okay for me to say, but you already have a job."

I had just won the Tony Award for playing Reno and was doing eight sold-out performances a week. He was recovering, looking for his next job, and suddenly had a lot of free time. We were seeing each other less and less, and I was resentful. And exhausted. And afraid of losing him.

That September, I suggested we go on a vacation. We needed time together. I had to figure out if this was going anywhere. We were on a Caribbean island when Hurricane Irene hit. If ever there was a sign! Looking back, I see how hard I was trying to make the relationship work despite the clues that it wasn't meant to be. I even thought that me being in *Anything Goes* was threatening to him, and I started to think that the only way forward was for me to quit—not him, but the show! I even called a meeting with the producers, sobbing, asking them if it was possible to get out of my contract. They told me, "We love you, but you can't quit!" I didn't—thank goodness—and when I look back on some of the things I did in my life, I'd say to my younger self, "Don't ever let a man get in the way of your career decisions."

That October, I got really sick. For the first time, it wasn't my voice. I could still sing, but I had no energy. Then I spiked a fever. I was so sick that I missed ten performances. It was bad. My mom emailed me, concerned: "Is Bobby taking care of you?"

He wasn't.

By then, I had switched agents and was working with Joe. It was still a new relationship, and so when he set me up on a lunch with my shero Amy Sherman-Palladino, the creator of *Gilmore Girls* (my all-time favorite show), I assumed it was because he wanted to impress me with his connections. (It worked!) I had no idea that Amy had written a new series called *Bunheads* and was vetting me to play the lead, Michelle. She never mentioned it at lunch. It was more of a meet and greet. After that, Joe sent me the script, and I wound up flying to LA that October to screen test, and then back again in November to shoot the pilot.

I was gone for three weeks, and I gave Bobby an ultimatum: when I returned, we'd either commit and move in together, as we had been talking about for a while. Or, we'd break up. Are we committed or not? What are we doing?

I flew back to New York that December, and right before Christmas he came to my apartment. I was really fighting for the relationship. I still wanted it to work. He did not.

His last words to me were "I just want to be alone."

And then he left.

I was devastated.

I thought that Bobby was the missing piece. But he wasn't. He taught me something, though. That I needed to find that piece in and for myself. That meant doing it alone.

I have no idea why, but I connected that realization to the black Hefty bag of granny squares that I had shoved in my closet two years earlier.

My relationship with Christian had torn me to pieces, but I'd be damned if I let Bobby do the same. I had some unfinished business to take care of.

I dumped all one hundred pieces on the floor and started to map them out, flower by flower, into a glorious garden. It was finally time to stitch them together.

BADASS

An Ode to Patti LuPone

The word *BADASS*, in all caps, is the first thing you see when you enter my apartment. It's a daily reminder of who I want to be. I created it by affixing thin strips of blue and purple craft paper to a large piece of plywood. The letters float on a colorful cloud of similarly cut pieces in pinks, reds, and oranges, which I like to think of as a striated sunset. When I created this collage, I was newly single and had just moved to LA to film *Bunheads*, my first television series. Amy Sherman-Palladino had asked me to play Michelle, an aging (at the geriatric age of thirty-five) ballerina turned Vegas showgirl who marries a man on a whim and winds up running her mother-in-law's dance studio after her husband suddenly dies.

The chance to work with Amy was enough for me to say yes, but I also connected deeply to the character of Michelle. In the script, she was looking for a fresh start. In many ways, I was too: I was thirty-six years old and heartbroken. I had been doing live theater for close to two decades and was looking for new challenges. I was ready for my own reinvention.

It all felt very meant to be when I found a 1969 A-frame Laurel Canyon bungalow with an airy loft: perfect for an art studio. After so many years of keeping all of my craft supplies in various Tupperware bins, canvas totes, and Hefty bags stuffed in a closet, I finally had a place to spread out. It was in this bungalow that I made the collage that has since become my daily affirmation.

For me, being a badass meant owning my talent and my major life decisions—not waiting until I was in a relationship, or more "settled down," whatever that even means. I had unknowingly started to take ownership of my actions when I bought the lake house and accepted the role of Reno. But something about buying that bungalow after spending six months in LA felt undeniably like a badass move! The lake house felt comfortable because my brother lived nearby, and Reno was challenging, but I played her on the Broadway stage, where I had a history. In LA, nothing was certain, but I claimed my place there anyway. I'm sure some people might have considered it rash or unnecessary, but for the first time in my life, I didn't care. I had always depended on the permission and approval of others — it was exhausting. It finally clicked with me that life didn't have to be that way.

That revelation was part of a long journey that started with Patti LuPone. In my mind, no one epitomizes a badass more than her.

I first saw her perform when I was sixteen years old and sitting in my living room in Troy, Michigan. It was December 1992, and she was performing in PBS's *Great Performances* series, which I watched with my mother, who was by no means your typical stage mom.

She didn't fawn or fuss over me, though she did find every theatrical opportunity for me as a child, starting with that *Annie* audition in Augusta. When we moved to Detroit, and I didn't get cast in the Boulan Park Middle School production of *Oliver!*, she searched for a "professional children's theater" and found the Peanut Butter Players, who not only let me perform in musicals like *The Wizard of Oz* and *The Wind in the Willows*, they paid me fifty dollars a week to do it! By then, we had become a die-hard musical theater family, but we had never visited New York City and our only access to Broadway was through TV, records, and cassette or VHS tapes. I had amassed quite the collection of cast albums— or "original Broadway cast recordings," if you want to be official. If a show was nominated for best musical in the late eighties or early nineties, then I *had* to have the album.

On this particular night, my mom and I were watching *Sondheim: A Celebration at Carnegie Hall*, which aired on PBS. I didn't know much about Sondheim beyond the song "There Won't Be Trumpets" from the musical *Anyone Can Whistle*, which I had sung for auditions because I had a big voice. I could hit all the high notes, but I had no clue what the song was about or why Sondheim was such a big deal.

And then Patti LuPone emerged on my television screen, wearing an *extremely* low-cut gold brocade pantsuit with major shoulder-pad action. I immediately recognized her—not from *Evita*, for which she had won the Tony in 1980, or even as Reno in *Anything Goes*, who she famously played on Broadway in 1987, but from the television series *Life Goes On*. On that show, she played the mom to a boy with Down syndrome, and I knew that she sang the show's theme song, "Ob-La-Di, Ob-La-Da." When she took center stage, the audience burst into applause, but instead of acknowledging that, or them, she just closed her eyes and began to sing. I was mesmerized. She was not just singing the song—she was *embodying* it, equal parts bold and vulnerable, sexy and intimate. There was something simultaneously terrifying and thrilling about her confidence. I'd never seen anything like it.

It was also the very first time I heard "Being Alive," from *Company*: "Somebody crowd me with love, somebody force me to care."

Even at sixteen, I intuited that the song was about embracing life. The messiness of it, the good, the bad, the ugliness of it. It was about leaping toward opportunities, not running away. Being afraid but doing it anyway. I didn't know it then, but I can see now how my mother's agoraphobia was just beginning to take hold of her around this time. She had stopped driving and grocery shopping. Her only friend was my Aunt Mary Anne. I was sixteen, and it already seemed to me that my own struggles with fitting in were more severe than those of my peers. I mean, I did have friends (though I wasn't popular), but I always felt awkward and out of place unless I was on a stage. That was my safe space, my escape. I needed a script and direction, because I had no role models at home of how to relate to people. This song was like a war cry, especially the line, "Alone is alone, not alive..."

When Patti sang it, I felt that she was

looking right at me, full-throated and so powerful. This was someone who was so alive that I could feel her voice vibrating throughout my body like an electric current. Granted, by then, my face was also a foot from the screen, so that might have been static. But it *felt* as if Patti was summoning me.

I turned to my mother, who was sitting on the couch behind me. "What was that?!"

"You can do that," she responded coolly.

Could I, though? I wasn't so sure. I knew I *wanted* to do that, but I had no idea how. I loved musical theater, but I didn't have a mentor—someone to look up to, someone to emulate. Until I saw Patti.

I became such a fan that my parents bought me the official VHS recording of that concert *and* the CD. And funnily enough, I have no idea who else performed at that concert, because she was the only one I watched—over and over, hundreds of times.

Seeing Patti sing that night shifted something within me and put me on a path. She showed me, in that moment, that being a performer was about more than projection or hitting high notes. She made you feel the meaning behind the music. When I asked her, years later, about what she was feeling before she took the stage, she said in a very matter-of-fact way, "It was my turn to sing."

Long before I knew the term "badass," I developed an understanding of what it meant just by studying Patti. She was confident and unapologetic about her talent, at a time when I was apologizing for everything—to the point that Jo Anne Lamun, who ran the Peanut Butter Players, forbade me from saying "I'm sorry" because I was doing it so often.

We were living in Detroit by then, but my parents were Southerners through and through, and I was raised to be a good little Southern girl. A Georgia peach. Humble. Nice and always polite. My father didn't mind moving to Michigan, but my mother found Northerners brash and brazen. Too outspoken and honest. Southerners might not like you, but they would never say it to your face—that would be impolite! (Have you heard the phrase "Bless your heart"? I can guarantee if a Southerner is saying that to you, it is not a compliment.) "Be careful," my father always said. My mother preferred "Remember where you came from." I still to this day say "Yes, ma'am" and "No, ma'am." In fact, when *Thoroughly Modern Millie* performed on the *Today* show in 2002, Katie Couric asked me a question and I replied, "No, ma'am." She said, "You don't have to call me ma'am." I said, "My mom would kill me if I didn't call you ma'am."

That was how I was raised, and for years, it was how I approached my career. Sure, I had a natural singing voice and had been studying dance since I was four years old, but I also "yes, ma'amed" my way through my early career, all the way up to Millie. I related to her wide-eyed enthusiastic and adventurous spirit—but not the "find and marry a wealthy husband" part, which was ultimately her goal. I credit my mother for instilling in me, from a very early age, the importance of financial independence. I started making money at age fourteen, with the Peanut Butter Players, and paid for my only year at college with earnings from the *Will Rogers* tour. But *Millie* was the first time that a show's success depended largely on me, and I had not yet figured out how to differentiate my own self from the character I was playing—or how to sing eight shows a week without blowing out my voice. That was why, as I mentioned earlier, I sought out the voice coach Joan Lader.

One day during *Millie*, I was finishing up a lesson with Joan, when her buzzer rang.

"I'll get it!" I said.

I went to open the door, and in walked Patti fucking LuPone!

Standing there, in her chic coat, with her purse slung over her shoulder, I saw the sparkle in her big, dark-brown eyes and felt electricity course throughout my body like it had ten years prior, in my living room, my face pressed to the television.

"Oh my God, Patti LuPone," I gasped. "Hello! Um…my name is Sutton Foster…"

"I know who you are," she said, kindly stopping me midsentence.

WTF! "Oh, okay, wow. Um…I just have

to say that you are the reason I'm in musical theater."

She looked at me, one eyebrow raised, slightly amused. Clearly, I was not the first person to tell her this.

"I saw you perform on the Sondheim celebration at Carnegie Hall," I continued, the words coming out in a nervous mix of halting and rapid-fire. "Well, I watched it on my TV and then wore out my CD of the concert listening to you sing 'Being Alive.'" She was still standing in the doorway, and while I knew I should move to the side to *let her in*, I couldn't stop the stream of words flowing from my mouth: "And that performance alone is why I wanted to be a performer. I just think you are amazing and thank you."

She stared me up and down and laughed, much like she did when the audience burst into applause at the end of her performance of "Being Alive."

"Well, thank you, Sutton," she said, and gave me a big hug.

I would like to think I melted into that hug, but I'm certain I was wound so tight that I just froze. She then headed in to her lesson.

I left Joan's studio and burst into tears in the lobby. Patti LuPone knew who I was! *And hugged me!* And she also went to the same vocal coach! Suddenly, my idol went from being my north star to being in my orbit. Maybe, just maybe, I was more like Patti than I thought was possible.

Cut to 2010, when the Roundabout Theatre Company wanted me to play Reno in their revival of *Anything Goes*. Patti LuPone's version of Reno was legendary—one of her most beloved performances ever, right up there with *Evita*. I hadn't seen her in the musical when she did it on Broadway, but I did see her perform the title number on the 1988 Tony Awards, and of course I had the cast recording. I had also, by then, seen her perform live in the revival of *Sweeney Todd*—and even went backstage to say hello. Over time, we had become friendly through various Broadway events.

So when my agent first approached me to play Reno, my gut reaction was *yes*. It felt meant to be! I didn't think about whether or not I could pull Reno off. I simply approached this role with the same "yes, ma'am" gusto I had used to approach all the other roles I had played in my career. But Reno, I soon learned, was not like the other characters. Like Patti, Reno walks into a room confident. Alive. All eyes on her. And she *enjoys* it. Patti fully embodied this. She's the star of the show, on and off the stage. As an actress, I knew better than to mimic another performance, especially one like Patti's. The shoes felt impossible to fill. I needed new shoes.

Joel Grey was my costar. In *Anything Goes*, he played the gangster Moonface Martin, and he is most famous for playing the Emcee in *Cabaret* on Broadway and in the movie, for which he won both a Tony Award *and* an Oscar. He turned eighty during *Anything Goes*. Talk about a role model! Singing "Friendship," one of my all-time favorite duets, with him remains a highlight of my career. He's the perfect player—always lobbing the ball back at you and keeping you on your toes. We became great friends during the show and still are.

He was also the first person to say what everyone else knew: I was struggling to find Reno. The rehearsal process was very sludgy. The music was familiar—I could hit all the notes—but the words felt clunky coming out of my mouth. It felt like I was wearing my mom's oversized clothes and shoes, playing pretend. Accessing Reno felt impossible. She was ballsy. The kind of woman who stands in the middle of a party and laughs too loudly. The one who wears low-cut dresses and loves being adored. She was everything I was not, and I couldn't figure out how to play her, which was a new experience for me. This was my tenth Broadway show, and I had won a Tony. I should have been able to figure this out on my own. It was starting to dawn on me that I was in over my head.

We rehearsed at Studio 54, which was where the revival of *Cabaret* had played. On a break one afternoon during rehearsals, Joel and I were sitting in the back of the auditorium when he looked at me with his impish smile and said, "When I was in rehearsals for the Emcee, I had no idea what I was doing. I had to figure out why I took the role in order to do the role." Then he looked me straight in the eyes and said, "Sutton, why did you take this part?"

I felt my chest tighten.

"Okay, everybody, break is over," our stage manager said.

I was so relieved to be interrupted, because I knew Joel was on to me, and in truth, I had no idea how to answer his question. At that time, I might have said, "Um...because Patti LuPone played it?"

I could answer that question for Millie: I was the bright-eyed optimist coming to New York to follow a dream! Same with Star to Be in *Annie*: "NYC! Just got here this morning! Three bucks, two bags, one me!" As Princess Fiona in *Shrek*, I could read the lines cold off the page and nail it, because I played the ogre princess at a time when I was waiting for my Prince Charming to come rescue me. I understood what that felt like. But Reno was an alien to me. I started having flashbacks to playing Marty when I was twenty-one and in the touring company of *Grease*—when I was literally fired because I had no idea how to play a tough, wise-cracking Pink Lady. Could the same thing happen on Broadway?

Actors often talk about the fraud factor: we're all so afraid that people will realize we don't actually know what we're doing. We spend a lot of time living in this ambiguous place of discovery where you have to fail in order to succeed. I was simply *flailing*.

On my way home from a tech rehearsal, right before we started previews, I was walking through Times Square when I called my agent, Steven, in a panic. "I will not fail! I will not fail!" I screamed into the phone. I thought I was going to be fired or, if not, then definitely panned in the *New York Times* when the show finally opened. I thought I was already letting everyone down—the cast, director, and producers—and was destined to ruin my career. The truth was, I desperately wanted to quit. That would have been easier.

Instead, my agent waited for my rant to subside and suggested I reach out to Larry Moss. I had heard about Larry from other theater friends. He was an acting coach, but really more of a therapist. He famously worked with Hilary Swank on *Boys Don't Cry* and with Helen Hunt in *As Good as It Gets*—both women won Oscars for their performances.

Larry helped me find Reno's humanity. He made me go beyond that façade and ask, "Why is she this way?" I had no idea. He kept pushing. Finally, I got so upset that I literally stomped my foot and blurted, "I don't like women like that! I don't know how to play her because I don't like her!"

At that moment, Larry pointed at me and said, "There it is. Why?"

I froze up. I didn't have an immediate answer. Why *didn't* I like her? What was the hurdle? What was holding me back? Why was I so afraid to embody her? Were these my feelings or my mother's? "Be good. Be nice. Be humble."

I was finally playing a character who demanded to take up space and made people uncomfortable. I didn't know how to play her because for so many years, I had done exactly the opposite! While I could belt things out onstage with the best of them, in my personal life, I kept myself, and my voice, small, so as to not intimidate anyone. Even the characters I chose reflected this. I would play the self-deprecating goofball to make people comfortable and use humor to deflect. Reno took the opposite approach: she was a woman who insisted on doing things her way.

Larry pushed me to ask, "Why does she behave this way? What is she hiding?"

One day, it clicked: she wants love. Attention is one kind of love—but Reno really wants unconditional love. Once I recognized that her façade was not her truth, I could play her. I finally understood that we both wanted the same thing, we just came at that shared desire in polar opposite ways.

Larry came to see me in dress rehearsal. I was feeling a little bit better, but I knew that I still wasn't wearing the character, the character was wearing me. It was frustrating—I could hear myself saying the lines, like I was still outside of her, instead of living them, like she was in my skin. I tiptoed at first.

For our first preview, in front of a live audience, I walked out onstage in a delicious gold beaded top and a brown skirt with a high slit, a faux-fur wrap draped over my shoulders. I had to sit at the bar and cross my legs.

The bartender said, "What'll it be, Reno?"

My line was: "A martini. But make it with rye and put a cherry in it instead of an olive."

When he handed me the Manhattan, I was shaking so badly that the drink splashed over the edge.

Still, the audience responded positively. That was because the last song in the first act is a huge, eight-minute tap dance number to "Anything Goes," in which I sang the lead and danced with the company. By the end of it, I had to turn my back to the audience just to catch my breath before I swung back around to belt the last line, arms flung in the air. It was a thrill to do, and the audience would always go wild. Kathleen Marshall, the director and choreographer, gave me the greatest gift by having this version of Reno dance with the ensemble.

Larry came to another preview, and on

that night, we got a standing ovation. I was beginning to gain confidence and was just outside my dressing room when Larry came barreling around the corner, his finger thrust out and pointing at me. "Stop apologizing!" he practically shouted. "You have to come onstage with the confidence you had at the end of your second act number! You have to take control from the minute you hit the stage, knowing that the audience already loves you! You have to own it!"

My heart was pounding.

He was right: I was still holding back. I was starting at zero, and he wanted me to start at nine.

"Enter the stage as if you had just received a standing ovation," he continued. "*Own it!*"

I thought of Patti LuPone walking on that stage at Carnegie Hall, in full control. It was her turn to sing.

I thought, *Why am I so afraid of this? Nothing bad will happen if I allow myself to be big. To be bold and strong and powerful. To be a badass.*

It was *my* turn to sing.

My heart was still pounding as I marched into my dressing room and wrote NO APOLOGIES and BADASS in lip liner on my dressing room mirror.

I needed to claim it.

From that moment on, I took Larry's note to heart and started dialing up every performance. I was on the fifty-yard line, and I had to get to the goal before opening night.

That night, I walked out in my first scene. Sat at the bar. Tossed off my faux fur. Crossed my legs. Lounged across the bar. Grabbed my Manhattan and my hand didn't shake. *There she is!* I thought. *I found her!*

Finally, I *was* Reno. Everything fell into place, and the cast felt it as much as I did. When the audience erupted into a standing ovation that night, I felt like I finally deserved it.

As I was in a car on my way to the after party that same night, my agent called me. "You just got a love letter from the *New York Times*," he said.

I hadn't read a review since I did *Millie*, and I still haven't read the one for *Anything Goes* in its entirety. I was excited and relieved, but I also realized that it didn't matter. I had this strange sense of peace about all of it, because I had found her. In the fucking nick of time.

One night, not long after we opened, I noticed that everyone in the ensemble was acting a bit weird. Like they had a secret. I soon figured out why: Patti LuPone was in the audience. I felt her presence, but I didn't know where she was sitting until the end of the performance. Every night, we got standing ovations. On that particular night, there was a V shape in the center where people remained seated—right in front of Patti, who was sitting fifth row center. Everyone stood but the five rows in front of Patti LuPone. I wouldn't have stood up in front of Patti LuPone either!

After the show, she came backstage to see me.

By then, I had changed into gray jeans and a purple T-shirt, my long hair pulled back in a ponytail. Patti entered my dressing room and gushed. I honestly can't remember what she said because I think I blacked out.

And once again, after she left, I burst into tears.

It's not every day your idol comes to see you perform.

I remain to this day Patti LuPone's number one fan. She set me on my path. I have a photo of her congratulating me in my dressing room that night sitting on my desk. It is more important to me than any review.

Anything Goes opened in the spring of 2011, and I wound up switching agents. That was when I met Amy Sherman-Palladino who is, much like Patti, a trailblazer and a badass. (She has since won writing *and* directing Emmys for *The Marvelous Mrs. Maisel*, becoming the first woman to do both in the same year.) She had also just seen me as this glamazon in *Anything Goes*, so, when I showed up at Cafe Un Deux Trois in my natural jeans-and-sneakers state, my hair in a messy bun, I'm sure she thought, *Who is this weirdo?* And that was before I ordered the chicken fingers and fries off the kids' menu. After our lunch, my agent sent me the *Bunheads* script.

My experience as Reno helped me prepare for the role of Michelle. Though in many ways Michelle's life paralleled mine. I felt like she had been written for me. She was not Millie, or Star to Be, or Sandy, or Fiona. Michelle was messy and difficult. There's this great scene where she says, "I don't have that kid-friendly gene. I am all sharp corners and a pool with no cover." Reno helped me access the "not nice" parts of myself. And Michelle took that a step further—she wasn't nice, yet you still loved her.

I flew out to LA for a screen test. That in and of itself was thrilling. Other than the cameo I did years earlier on *Flight of the Conchords*, an episode of *Law & Order: SVU*, and an appearance on *Sesame Street* singing with Elmo, this was new. Not only was it not a one-off like those other parts, it was the *lead* in a series. I did the audition with Amy, a reader, and two other people. After I finished, Amy said, "We want you as Michelle!" I didn't realize how much I wanted it, how badly I craved a change, until that moment.

I had been playing Reno for a year—the role of a lifetime, so where does one go from there? I was at a point in my career where I could continue working on the stage and comfortably have a successful career. But at thirty-six years old, I didn't feel satisfied with that and was determined to make some strong, bold choices. I needed to test myself and find out what I was capable of. Entering the television world at my age was terrifying—but also exciting. And leaping into the Amy Sherman-Palladino universe was a dream come true.

Bunheads was filmed at the Sunset Gower Studios, where, one day, I spotted several large sheets of plywood poking out of a dumpster. I had been experimenting with collage on paper and thought it might be interesting to try it on wood. This was a riff on that missing shattered girl—but this time, I wanted to use paper, not glass. I lugged a 5½-by-2½-foot piece to my Mazda3 hatchback. It barely fit, and I had no idea what I was going to make with it. I just knew that it had to come home with me.

That evening, I propped the wooden

canvas up in my art studio against the slanted A-frame walls and pulled out all my bins of paper—craft, construction, and magazine tear sheets. I started with the pink, orange, and red hues, cutting long, thin strips, ¼ inch wide, in a repetitive motion. It felt like a form of meditation. I methodically affixed each paper ribbon to the wooden canvas with matte Mod Podge. The next time I looked up it was two a.m. This went on for days until I filled the entire panel.

Over and over, I would repeat this ritual: choosing the colors, cutting the strips, selecting the patterns. Deciding the pomegranate red worked best with the cotton-candy pink. Building the foundation. Gluing it down. Making a mistake. Undoing it, covering it up, or just letting it become part of the piece.

Once the background was complete, I made the letters. As the word BADASS slowly appeared on the canvas, I felt the sentiment emerge within me. I realized, during these late-night meditative sessions, that the quality I had always associated with Patti LuPone helped me find a feeling that had always been a part of me.

That said, as I continued to paste pieces down, I realized that Patti's version of badass was not necessarily mine. For me, it was not taking the stage at Carnegie Hall. It was auditioning for the Peanut Butter Players when I didn't get cast as Nancy in *Oliver!* It was going on tour with *The Will Rogers Follies* at the age of seventeen. It was not giving up after getting fired as Marty. It was turning down the chance to play Éponine in *Les Miz* on Broadway so I could be an understudy in *Millie*. It was never letting a "no" or a criticism deter me. It was all the ways in which I flung myself into these opportunities, knowing I had the talent and trusting, even as I leapt, that I could some-how pull it off. It was saying yes to Reno, and making my own version of her. It was moving to LA to play another messy charac-ter, but this time on TV. I had been doing badass things my whole life, but I never gave myself the credit. Instead I focused on the times when I had felt more unsure, the things I thought needed fixing.

This was not the only revelation. As I started making the letters, I also began to see how, in certain ways, my mom was a badass, too. She was the only one in her family to have left home. She advocated for both of her kids to be in the arts. She fought for me to have a different life than what was offered to her. In many ways, she saw the badass in me first, and pushed me to find it for myself. Patti LuPone was my north star, but my mother is responsible for me becoming my own late-bloomer badass.

My mantra, to this day, is: "I worked my entire life to be at this moment. I can allow this to be good." It gives me permission to own my talent. It calms me down. I don't have to apologize, make myself small. And I can still be nice while doing it.

For so many years, I wanted to be more like Patti. But as I glued the last strip to the collage, I realized, I needed to be more me.

There she is, I thought to myself, as I propped the final piece against the wall. *I found her.*

Two Badasses, Comparing Notes

In the fall of 2019, I was back in New York, married to Ted, and our daughter Emily was just about to start pre-K. The seventh season of *Younger* was slated to start in March of 2020, and I had also just been cast as Marian in *The Music Man* opposite Hugh Jackman. Life was pretty freaking great. I went out for dinner at the Mermaid Inn with my friend Sierra and saw that Dylan Passman, one of my old students from Ball State, where I had been teaching since 2010, was the host. As we were finishing up dinner, Dylan stopped by the table to say goodbye. He smiled wide, barely able to contain his excitement, and said, "Patti LuPone is in the back room."

I felt a giddy rush—even after all these years, I still feel the Patti effect. "Can you bring me to her to say hello?"

"Nothing in this world would give me greater pleasure," he said as he offered his arm to escort me.

Patti was having dinner with the actor John Cameron Mitchell and another friend, and she greeted me with the warmest smile and a big hug.

She said, "I am so excited about *Music Man*! When do you start?"

This was pre-pandemic, so the answer then was September 2020.

We then shot the shit in the back of the Mermaid Inn. It felt oddly comfortable and normal, if that's even possible. So much so that right before I left, I summoned the courage (or maybe it was the two glasses of wine?) to ask, "Can I get your number?"

We exchanged information, and while writing this chapter, I summoned my courage again.

"I am working on a book and you are a big part of it. A huge reason why I'm an actress," I wrote to her in a text. "Would you be open to an interview? With me?"

I was nervous as I hit Send, but then I thought, *The worst thing that could happen is she says no.*

That same day, I was in the parking lot of Target doing some last-minute Christmas shopping when I heard my phone ping. Patti had responded: "Hi Sutton! Of course. I'm honored. Xoxo"

Once again, I burst into tears, this time in my car.

Thirty years after seeing her on my TV

in Troy, Michigan, I spoke to Patti LuPone from my crafting/office room on Zoom and learned that we have more in common than I ever would have imagined. Here are some highlights from our conversation on December 26, 2020.

PL: What's the book about?

SF: How hobbies saved my life.

PL: (*Laughs*) I get asked often, "Patti, if you retire, what would you do?" I don't have a hobby. I tried gardening and I sprained something in my hands. I went to the doctor thinking it was carpal tunnel syndrome, and he said, "You have privileged hands." I got injured from weeding. I don't knit. Or paint. I do read a lot. But what I do has been my entire life. That weighs heavy on my mind. If I ever stopped performing, what would I do to stay mentally fit?

SF: That's what my book is about! All the ways in which crafting has helped me stay sane. It's my life seen through all the things I have made. I might cry when I talk right now, because I made this

giant collage that hangs in my hallway in
NYC. It says *BADASS*. You are my
number one badass. It was your performance in the Sondheim celebration in
1992 that made me want to do musical
theater for a living. I didn't understand
what I had just seen. You were this force.
Did you know a sixteen-year-old kid in
Troy, Michigan, would see you and lose
her mind?

PL: I was doing *Life Goes On* in
Los Angeles. It was the beginning of
hiatus, and I got a phone call about
performing for Stephen Sondheim's
birthday. I had recently auditioned for
Stephen to be Bernadette Peters's
replacement in *Sunday in the Park with
George*. At the audition, he saw me and
said, "I don't want a belter." And I
thought, *You don't like me. And that is
not the only thing I do.* I didn't get the
part and was brokenhearted. So I didn't
have a relationship with him. Or Scott
Ellis or Susan Stroman [who directed the
PBS special]. But I did with Paul
Gemignani, the conductor, because he

did *Evita*. I trusted him. So when I was asked to perform "Being Alive" for Stephen's birthday, I said yes.

I get overwhelmed, especially when I don't know the people I'm working with. I am a deer in headlights. So scared. I also know that I have been given a gift to sing full volume in an open space. It happened in *Evita*. That was when I realized, *This is why you're in Broadway musicals. This voice.* I realized what my gift was. What God had given me. I delighted in it.

I went out on the stage that evening in fear that I was going to forget the lines. Or not hit the high D note. But then, I just let it go. There is also something about singing with a full orchestra which blows me away. It is what I was built for. I love being one of the instruments. I want to figure out where I fit in with the sound. With Paul at the helm, I could relax.

SF: That song, "Being Alive," in particular resonated with me. My mom was agoraphobic. Oddly enough, she has two children who are Broadway actors and very much of the world. I have struggled with anxiety myself. So maybe it was a combination of you singing it and the power of the words. I now sing a version of it in my concerts because you sang it, but there is something about the cry to embrace the messiness of life that really strikes me. I want the sleepless nights. I want to feel it all. Not running away from life but wanting to dive into it.

PL: And the connection: we want to be loved. "Somebody hold me too close." Somebody know me. And care for me. So many things go on in your head as a performer. And you can still have an effect on an audience. That also may have been my debut at Carnegie Hall, which is an intimidating place. But I went out there. It was my turn, and I went out there.

SF: That is so great.

PL: Don't you sometimes feel like you're being fed to the lions? Especially when you have to perform in a big lineup of people. I feel like I'm going to fail, that

I'm not going to be good enough for the company I'm in. I also think, *Is the audience going to be with me?* Every night that I perform, I go and look at the audience. I want to see who I'm playing to. I look people in the eye during the show—so I pick one or two audience members to sing to. I don't want to be thrown during the performance, so I pick the one that is indifferent. And I play to him or her. You see it immediately. And you think, *Oh God, they hate me!* As opposed to the rest of the people, who don't necessarily hate me. I don't know if it's reinforcing my inferiority complex or if it's the stuff that makes me a performer. I have to go out there and get them. Maybe it's a psychological thing that I look for the one who's hard to get, and I get him.

    SF: Do you have a mantra?

    PL: I have a prayer I say before all performances: "Help me remember the lyrics." Then I thank all the gods and goddesses in the world that I am worthy of what I have and what I can relay.

   I also think about what Walter Bobbie

said to me at Encores at City Center, after I came back from a vocal cord operation: "You've got it. Now give it away." I love that. Of course.

That's what we're supposed to do as performers. There is no holding back. Maybe that's my mantra: "Give it away."

I was raised a Catholic, and while I don't practice at all, I still cross myself and pray before I go onstage. It's so funny, because in life, I'm scared of everything. I'm scared of the dark. Someone must have read me very scary books as a child, because I think the boogeyman is under my bed. If all the lights are out, I get into bed really quickly. 9/11 terrorized me. But I'm fearless onstage. I guess it's the only place I can be fearless—so I don't let myself down.

SF: I feel that way too! The stage is the one place where I am in complete control. I know if the spotlight light has been changed because it's a bit brighter. But in my real life, I'm like, *Ahhh!*

PL: The life fear has nothing to do with the stage fearlessness. David Mamet said, "Wipe your feet at the door! Don't bring the shit from your life onto the stage." How many times have we had to go onstage and say, "Get out of my way, I am here for a reason"? The badass comes from controversy. From obstacles. She comes to survive. I am not a badass in my life. But I won't let anyone fuck around with me onstage. I have said, "You can fuck with me in my real life, but not onstage."

SF: I have said that very same thing!

PL: We are very much alike, my dear. The stage is our special place. We have been gifted. It is not to be toyed with. I never know what to do in real life when people say something shocking. And then twenty minutes or three days later, I come up with the perfect retort— but never in the moment. In real life, I'm vulnerable and in shock. But onstage, I'm in control. Of course, some- one else has written the lines for me.

SF: You have an ownership on the stage

PL: So do you. You have a light around you. You own it! People always are shocked that I want to rehearse as much as I do. And I say, "That's because I don't want to stink onstage." I want the audience to relax. I want them to know that I got this. When I'm in the audience and see someone stumbling, I can't watch the play anymore. I'm nervous for that performer! I never want to be that performer.

SF: I have dreams where I'm on the stage and everyone is looking at me, waiting for me to do or say something, and I have no idea what I'm supposed to be doing.

PL: When I'm onstage, I feel as if I'm participating in good in the world. Contributing to the universe. Doing something positive. Even if I'm playing a villain. There is a risk in doing this work. Opening nights take minutes off of my life. First preview.

SF: Same! Who discovered your talent?

PL: My mother. She used to trick

me out to guests to do my Marilyn Monroe impersonation—as a four-year-old. I was precocious. I would drop my shirt off my shoulder and pout my lips. My dad was the principal of the elementary school in my hometown, and he started an afterschool program. There was a dance class taught by Miss Marguerite, so my mom enrolled me to give me something to do, and I fell in love with the audience. I never looked back. The voice was this big loud thing that was always there. I had to take piano lessons, and I was in chorus. And I joined the band because there were boys. Northport had a great music program. When we were in third grade, we were given an instrument to play. It was integral to our education—just like math was. I knew I was destined for the Broadway musical stage.

SF: Did you do youth theater?

PL: Yes, I was Rosie in *Bye Bye Birdie* and then I played Louise in *Gypsy* with the Patio Players. The Patio Players were teenagers from the high school music department, and putting on musicals with no adult supervision was our summer activity. Kids who just loved the stage.

SF: I was in the Peanut Butter Players!

PL: Then I went to New York City and I went to Broadway. When my mom and dad divorced, I said to my brother [also an actor], "We're free." My dad wanted us to be teachers.

SF: Did you have a Patti LuPone growing up?

PL: Bette Davis was my badass. And Edith Piaf. Her voice was not perfect. But you could hear the emotion in every word. Why do we do this? We do it to transport people. We don't do it for us, we do it for them. I would cut school if there was a new Bette Davis movie. She was not the most beautiful movie star, but she was the fiercest. There is something about her strength. It's a composure or sense of self.

SF: That is what you have: sense of self.

PL: Really? I'm glad you think so. I
know who I am and it is constantly evolv-
ing. It doesn't stay the same. But I think
the sense of self comes from one's experience in life. I say this without wanting to
evoke self-pity, but I come from the
school of hard knocks. I had to fight for
everything I've got. I have been un-
employed. I have been vilified. I have a
reputation, and while some of it may be
deserved, it was never about me. It was
always about the production. What we
were doing onstage. A lot of it comes
from survival. More often than not, I
fought to continue because I have a
God-given gift, and no one is going to
stop me from doing it. I have been kept
out of employment because casting
directors didn't like me, so they wouldn't
see me! Now I'm on the other side, but a
lot of the beginning of my career was
fighting to work. And then the critics
didn't like me. And I'd say, "Let them say
whatever—I have an audience who
wants to see me because I speak to something in their bodies that they relate to."

I wish I didn't have a hard-knock career, but I don't know where I would be if it was handed to me. I understand when actors are humiliated onstage. I understand fear. I've been through it. I've seen people who have had their careers handed to them—and I'm not sure they're as good.

SF: I love everything about you!

PL: I love everything about you, because we're the same person.

SF: What is your advice to young performers?

PL: That they should know their craft, starting with, that it is a craft. That takes study not only of the craft itself, but its history. Who came before you? Why are you here? Why are we here and what are we doing?

SF: I have work to do! What was your relationship like with your mom?

PL: Strained. I come from Italian immigrants—my parents were both first-generation American. Their parents were immigrants and didn't speak English. I'm 100 percent peasant. My mother didn't understand my brother's or my desire to be in this industry. They were not supportive growing up. I wanted to go to the school for performing arts. And she wouldn't let me go. It felt like a punishment. I was like, *Don't you see that I'm going to do this for the rest of my life?* There was a lot of strife. I left the house. When I could get out, I got out.

[*Young man enters room.*]

This is my son. Josh, say hello to Sutton Foster.

J: Hi, Sutton Foster.

PL: I'm going to cook fish. Honey, do you want the fish?

SF: Do you like to cook? Cooking is a hobby!

PL: Yes. But you have to practice.

SF: Patti, I am so grateful.

PL: I love you, and I love your talent. And I am so honored to be part of your process.

SF: I'm going to cross-stitch a poem. It's called "An Ode to Patti LuPone."

YOU ROCK

I got an email in June 2011 from my mom that simply said, "You rock."

I immediately burst out laughing.

This was right after I won the Tony for *Anything Goes*, and it was so very unlike her. It was the beginning of a two-year period where my mom started acting much nicer to me.

I have Xanax to thank for that.

My father told me, during interviews for this book, that the medication was originally prescribed to him to help him quit smoking. (It didn't work.) He said my mom wanted to try it for her anxiety, which she knew she suffered from, even though she was never officially diagnosed. My dad said she "loved it" and that she had even said, "I wish I had been taking this sooner."

That broke my heart. How I wish she had been taking it all along. How I wish she had gotten help earlier in her life. My dad told me that my mom had once talked about seeing someone and getting help, but she never did. I feel so sad about that missed opportunity. But I was grateful for this little glimmer of a happier mom.

That email inspired me to do another paper-on-wood collage similar to *BADASS*, but with the words *YOU ROCK*. For this one, I used two large pieces of plywood. I wanted it to be really big so I could remember those words and this time in my relationship with my mother.

There were other things that made this a sunny and optimistic period in my life: I had begun filming the first season of *Bunheads* and was loving my single life in LA. I wrote my mom an email during this period that said, "I don't miss New York at ALL! I think I'm meant to live in the sunshine. I don't think I've ever quite felt 'at home' in my adult life...with touring and even in New York. But I feel it now. It's crazy!"

Filming *Bunheads* was a radically different experience than live theater. My days started with the sun—a hint of orange on a dark periwinkle horizon. I would splash cold water on my face, choke down some coffee, grab my dog Linus, and plop him in the front seat of Dolly, my dolphin-gray Mazda3 hatchback. Then I'd drive from Burbank to the *Bunheads* set on Sunset Gower, watching the sun rise in the rearview mirror. I'd meet my ballet teacher Jackie at six a.m. in my dressing room, where Amy had asked me to choose the wall color (pale yellow, my favorite) and had a ballet barre installed. I spent the first hour of every day trying to get into "ballet" shape, which was harder than I anticipated. I'm more of a tap dancer, which I had been doing as Reno for over a year! The last time I had taken ballet was in college, so we did a full warm-up of pliés and tendus, ronds de jambe, and developpés every day. My thirty-six-year-old body was not as flexible as it had been in my teens and twenties—

it ached its way through each move. It was humbling, painful, and beautiful to revisit something that had been such a huge part of my life when I was younger. I even bought a brand-new pair of pink Capezio ballet shoes and sewed on the straps, just like my mom had done for me as a kid!

I'd next head to the hair and makeup trailer to begin the transformation into Michelle, and then I'd be driven to set for rehearsal of the first scene of the day. (Fun fact: *Scandal* was shooting on the same lot, so every day I'd wave to Tony Goldwyn and Kerry Washington from our respective golf carts.)

The biggest challenges for me were how many lines I had to learn (there were *a lot*, and they changed daily) and the schedule (the days were *long*). Amy Sherman-Palladino is known for her rapid-fire dialogue, filled with pop culture references and sarcastic humor. Her characters are lovable and flawed and often have complicated relationships with their mothers or mother figures. True to form, the *Bunheads* scripts had a lot of words on the page, which I needed to know verbatim and say *fast*. In the theater, we had weeks of rehearsal for one scene, but on TV, we'd rehearse for ten minutes. That's why I was constantly practicing my lines with the production assistants, script supervisor, or fellow actors—because once we stepped on set to rehearse the scene, I had to make quick, hopefully smart choices, and then stick to them. Someone would lay down a mark, and all the lights—and camera—would focus on me, at *that* mark. In those early days, the camera assistants surrounded my marks with small sandbags, used for novice TV actors like me who would overshoot their mark. This way, I'd end up in the right place without having to look down.

Amy was also known for filming scenes in one shot—rather than using close-ups—which meant there was nowhere to hide. That felt like theater, and I particularly loved filming the dance sequences. There was one in which Fanny (Michelle's mother-in-law, played by the incredible Kelly Bishop) was teaching a ballet class in her dance studio, which was lined with mirrors—a nightmare for filming. Chris, our brilliant camera operator, danced right along with us, holding the Steadicam as everyone swirled and danced around him. He did all this and still managed to dodge his reflection in the many mirrors. Those are some skills right there! Go watch this scene! Better yet, watch the whole series because it's *really* fantastic (and not just because I was in it).

The other big difference between being on a set versus being onstage was that someone was always following me around. That totally freaked me out. In theater, you're responsible for getting your ass to the stage for your cues. No one escorts you anywhere. But on a TV set, someone would literally broadcast over a walkie-talkie when I had to go pee. The lingo is "10-1," but I refused to say this code. Instead, I would loudly announce, "I gotta go pee!"

Another big difference? Snacks. For more than two decades, I brought my own water and snacks and whatever the hell else I needed. On set, someone brings you whatever you could possibly want—because they don't want you wandering off! I was always going rogue because I wasn't used to people keeping tabs on me.

The last big difference was the "hurry up and wait" principle. You rehearse for ten minutes, then they light and set up for twenty minutes, then you shoot for ten minutes, then they move the cameras and lights to another setup. In those early days of shooting, I would just sit in my cast chair eating granola bars.

Working with Kelly Bishop was a lifesaver. She played Lorelai's mother on *Gilmore Girls* and was Sheila in the original Broadway production of *A Chorus Line*. She is a broad through and through — and she taught me how to navigate this new world.

"Don't focus on learning the entire script," she advised early on. "Prep for what you need to do three days ahead. Learn it in little chunks. And when you're done filming a scene, let it go and move on."

It was a lot to learn at the age of thirty-seven (I had a birthday in March), but it was exhilarating. I would come home after a sixteen-hour day of shooting, exhausted and brain-fried but ridiculously happy.

On the weekends, I would sit outside in the seventy-degree weather, sipping rosé, learning lines, and throwing squeaky balls to Linus. He'd come with me to set every single day and stay with Brenda, the wardrobe supervisor. She got him a little bed and twenty squeaky balls, which he would chase between people's legs during their fittings. Whenever he got a little smelly, the groomer van would come to the lot and spruce him up. Linus was loved by everyone.

Perhaps my most surreal moment happened one Saturday, when I was driving to a dance rehearsal for a tap sequence on the show. I stopped dead in my tracks on Laurel Canyon Boulevard, at the corner of Moorpark. There was a giant billboard of me lounging on the ground in a tank top and shorts, with four toe-shoed ballet girls standing behind me and the title *Bunheads* in big red letters, floating beside my head. It felt different from seeing my face as Reno on the side of a bus or on a billboard in Times Square. I wasn't hidden beneath a wig and costume. This time it felt like *me* up there—and I was about to appear on television screens in people's living rooms. Including my parents'.

My mom and I were emailing almost every day. The night before the show premiered she wrote, "I hope *Bunheads* is a smashing success." By then, she was also on Facebook anonymously—Hunter and I were her only two friends—so she could further keep tabs on what we were up to.

With *Bunheads*, she could also watch me perform without having to leave her house. After every episode, she'd write me to say how much she loved it (though she also wrote that she had to put the subtitles on because we all talked way too fast). She sent me articles about the series that she found online, and I'd send her pictures of me on set, or of artwork that I was working on, or of Linus being adorable.

Michelle had a fractured relationship with her mother on the show. She also had a brother, and Amy cast Hunter to play him! He was still living in New York, doing more writing and directing than acting. He flew out to LA for the job and we did some great scenes together, including a version of "You Belong to Me." We both sang, and I played the ukulele! My mom got to watch her two children act together on the screen. She emailed, "Loved *Bunheads* tonight seeing you and Hunter working together and singing too. Love you, Mom."

By then, my mom and Hunter were speaking again. After *Urinetown*, he did a Broadway production of *Little Shop of Horrors* that had a soft opening in Coral Gables, and my parents decided to get tickets. My brother said they spent the afternoon together as if nothing had happened. It was like they had an unspoken truce to bury the hatchet.

Thanks to therapy, I realized that was their story, not mine! I quit right before I moved to Los Angeles because I finally accepted my mother and stopped trying to change her—and it seemed that she had finally accepted me.

This period with Hunter was special too. It reminded me of that four-day cross-country trip we had taken all those years earlier. Hunter stayed with me and slept in the loft with all of my artwork, including the *BADASS* collage, which was leaning against the wall. We made fish tacos and guacamole from my avocado tree, and he bought me a grill for the backyard, and we watched *Homeland* and went on a hike together. I felt more grounded than I had ever been.

After *Bunheads* wrapped its first season, a friend reached out and asked, "Where are you on the dating scene?" I had maybe gone on two dates since the Bobby breakup and was super indifferent. In truth, I had boarded up my heart with steel gates and nails. Closed up tight. I wasn't interested in falling in love or being in a relationship. I really didn't care.

My friend asked if he could give my number to a friend, a director and screenwriter. I said, "Sure."

That same day, I heard the ping of a new text: "Hi, It's Ted." It was the screenwriter/director. "This is what I look like." And he sent a photo of Zero Mostel.

I laughed out loud.

I sent him back a Google image of an old woman with no teeth and said, "This is me."

He asked me on a date, but I said, "I am very busy. I only have Tuesday from 2:30 to 3:30 available."

We were finishing up *Bunheads*, but honestly, I was just not interested.

He took the date.

We met for coffee at a restaurant on Ventura Boulevard in Los Angeles called Kings Road. I got there early and grabbed a table. In walked a very tall, handsome man, wearing a blue puffer jacket even though it was eighty degrees outside. As we talked, he shared a few personal things, like the death of his father the year before, and a major job that he had been fired from—let's just say I was impressed by his candor. I liked how honest and self-deprecating he was. He made me laugh. He also clearly loved theater but was not a *fan*—there is a difference. He wasn't a stage-door Johnny. He didn't see me as a Broadway persona. He admitted that he listened to the Broadway channel on Sirius XM but that he couldn't carry a tune. He also told me that he and his dad had seen me in *The Drowsy Chaperone* when it played the Ahmanson Theatre in Los Angeles back in 2005.

"You had a broken wrist, right?" he asked.

I did! And I laughed thinking back to that moment in my life. I had slipped and fallen while rehearsing a song called "Accident Waiting to Happen." (You can't make it up!) I almost went back to New York in my cast to heal as I had another number called "Show Off," in which I had to do crazy gymnastic tricks. Rather than sit out the show, I taught myself how to do one-handed cartwheels.

Ted told me that his dad loved the movies and that when he was a kid he memorized every Oscar winner for every year.

"1975?" I quizzed him.

"*Cuckoo's Nest* won best picture. Nicholson won actor. Louise Fletcher won actress. George Burns supporting actor, and Lee Grant supporting actress," he said without missing a beat.

Man, he was cute.

On our second date, he took me to a putt-putt place in the Valley. We now call this our *Karate Kid* date, as it reminded us of when Daniel takes Ali to Golf N' Stuff. On every hole, Ted said we got to ask each other a question. Neither of us wanted the date to end, so as he was driving me back to my house we stopped at a dive bar on Ventura and kept asking each other questions over Manhattans.

"What is your least favorite trait about yourself?" I asked.

"I can be a snob," he said.

I appreciated his honesty.

Then he said, "What's yours?"

"I'm a control freak," I said.

We both entered the relationship with self-awareness of the good and the bad.

On our third date, I asked him why he had never been married or lived with someone. He told me that he had been too career-focused and truly felt like he hadn't met the person he wanted to do that with.

Still, we didn't kiss until our fifth date — and that was after a breakfast date. He was concerned that we were going to end up in the friend zone. Honestly, I was still scared. My heart was so guarded. We went to a place called Sweet Butter, and I told him I was free until 2:00 p.m., so afterward he drove me to a look-out point on Mulholland and we kissed in the car. After eggs.

Everyone always told me that the right man would come along when I wasn't looking for it, and that's exactly what happened. Ted was different from any of the other men I had dated. He was confident and self-assured. Goofy and incredibly smart. Accomplished and not threatened by my career. I felt completely myself around him. And I could see how he could fit into my world. Our romance escalated quickly.

I wanted everyone in my life to meet him. When I introduced him to Stephanie one night over dinner, she followed me into the bathroom, and as I was peeing, she said, "You can't mess this up! We love him!" She saw how Ted folded seamlessly into whatever environment I brought him into. She could see how comfortable and assured I was around him.

Megan was in town visiting her family in

Pasadena, and I remember calling her on the phone and saying, "I think this is it!"

I invited her to come watch the Oscars with us, specifically to meet Ted. When he arrived, he sat on the couch, and Linus curled up at his feet. Megan and I locked eyes—she knew that Linus was my barometer. It was a sign.

On my thirty-eighth birthday, Ted surprised me with a trip to Disneyland. It was just the two of us, and he got me a *Happy Birthday Sutton* button, which I wore all day. Ted had grown up in Southern California, and he took me to all his favorite spots in the park. We got beignets and mint juleps in the French Quarter and rode the Matterhorn at night. It was really sweet and romantic.

On March 19, I sent my mom an email: "Hey! I've started dating someone. He's a director/writer that a fellow producer friend of mine introduced to me. We've been dating since the end of January. It's been very slow and easy and very nice. I really like him. Smart, funny, tall... handsome... generous, successful and a gentleman. He's 42, never been married. We had a fantastic day. I'm just taking it nice and slow. Love you."

She responded, "I am glad you have someone to spend your birthday with. Does he have a name?"

She was deft with Google and Facebook by then. I knew better than to fall for that!

"His name is Theodore," I responded.

She wrote back, "No last name?"

Early that summer, Michael Rafter and I were working on a concert series and were hired as the entertainment on a gay cruise with two thousand gay men on a boat. I brought Julien as my guest, and we laughed about how you couldn't pay me to get in the pool with two hundred hunky gay men looking for a good time. We had a ball! The cruise went to Singapore, Vietnam, and then Hong Kong, where it ended due to engine trouble. I was literally on a slow boat to China.

I spent that entire trip emailing back and forth with Ted. It was actually nice to have a little distance, as things were getting more hot and heavy. Every day he would send me a little video clip of something he found beautiful or funny. My favorite was the Firebird Suite animated in *Fantasia 2000* (if you've never seen it, watch it immediately). I was in the South China Sea watching *Terriers*, the show Ted had created before I met him, and he was back in LA watching *Bunheads*.

When I got back to the States in May, I did a concert with Michael at Feinstein's at the Nikko in San Francisco. Ted met me there, and we spent the weekend in Napa Valley. This was a turning point in our relationship. Was I falling in love? Or did I have to run? My heart was still thawing, but Ted was so patient. He had the "Four Ps": he was Patient, he was Persistent, he Picked me up, and he always Paid.

That weekend, we both said, "I love you."

In April, Ted and I flew to New York and stayed at the Empire Hotel. I had been asked to announce the 2013 Tony nominations.

My mother sent me this email message: "Have fun in New York. Looking forward to the Tony nominations. Introduce Ted to your brother. Love you, Mom."

I wrote her back and simply said, "You rock."

OWL BLANKET

That August, my phone rang. It was my dad.

"Sutton," he said, sounding oddly distant. "Your mom is sick."

That explained why I hadn't heard from her in a while. Between falling in love and working, I had been so busy that I hadn't realized it had been months since I received an email.

"Is she okay?" I asked.

"She's in the hospital," he replied, in a very matter-of-fact way. "She passed out at home, so I called the ambulance. They think she had a stroke."

He sounded almost robotic, which worried me all the more. I knew he was hiding something.

"I'll be on the next plane," I said.

"She doesn't want you to know," he said. "She'll be mad if you come."

His voice was getting emotional, finally. I knew he needed me to be there, and that she had forbidden him from asking me to come. She was extremely private about her health. She had actually spent two weeks in the hospital with extreme abdominal pain a couple years prior, though I didn't learn about it until a year later when my dad let it slip. (It turned out to be diverticulitis—unfortunately caused by tomato seeds. After that diagnosis, she was never again allowed to eat those tomato sandwiches that had remained a staple all her life.)

I don't know why she was so secretive—perhaps she didn't want me to worry about her—but that was why, when my dad called me this time, I knew it was bad.

I didn't give myself time to think or feel. I just jumped into action and booked a ticket for the very next day. I called my dad to let him know I was on my way, and he kept saying over and over, "She doesn't want you to know." And I was like, "Fuck that, I'm coming."

I flew to Florida the next day and drove straight to the hospital. My dad met me in the lobby. He looked scared and defeated. We stayed quiet in the elevator.

When I walked into the room and saw my mom, I gasped. I hadn't seen her in two years, since the time I visited with Bobby. She looked so tiny and frail, ensnared in a tangle of wires and lines, hooked up to IVs and machines. Her veins were bright blue against the gray, almost translucent pallor of her skin.

As soon as she spotted me, her body tensed up as she shouted, "What the hell are you doing here?" The angry outburst startled the nurse. Her eyes darted to my father. "Bobby! Bobby! Why the hell is she here?"

My dad hung his head.

She kept saying, "I'm pissed!" over and over again through clenched teeth, nostrils flared. "I'm pissed!"

I was unfazed—and determined. When Dada behaved this way, I left the room. But with her, I stayed. I was no longer afraid. I just pulled up a chair, looked her straight in her eyes, and said, "Well, I'm not going anywhere, and you're attached to wires, so you're not either."

It was the first time I ever had a leg up on my mother. She was trapped, and it infuriated her. Even if someone unhooked her from all those beeping machines, she was too weak to walk without someone helping her. Of course, this further enraged her.

"Feel the feelings, but I'm not leaving," I said.

By then, I was living by the mantra "Acceptance without expectations," and that allowed me to stay in a relationship with my mother. Still, in that moment, I thought, *Wow! All that energy and anger is actually impressive. She's still got it!*

The difference was that she couldn't hurt me with it anymore. After so many years of therapy and insisting on staying in her life despite her terrible behavior, I was beginning to see how it was her façade. The kind emails over the past two years especially had given me a glimpse of who she could be, and what our relationship might become.

I looked around the room, and it made me so sad. It was pitiful. No flowers or cards. No one knew she was sick but me and my dad. She had completely isolated herself from everyone, including her own children.

"Dad, you have to tell Hunter what's going on," I said in the hallway, out of her earshot. "He needs to be here."

He agreed and called him right there, from the hall.

I was groggy from the red-eye and still had no idea what had caused my mother to pass out in the first place. I finally learned from a doctor who was making rounds that she hadn't had a stroke: it was melanoma that had metastasized. The original tumor, the doctor explained, was on her thigh and was the size of a grapefruit. That led to more tumors in her brain, which caused her to faint.

"What?" I said, trying to imagine how that was possible.

The nurse read my mind, adding, "I've never seen anything like it! Why did she let it get so big?"

My parents had not shared a bed or bedroom for decades; I assumed that she had somehow kept it hidden from my father. I wasn't sure how, but I wasn't going to try to explain any of that to the nurse. I also felt guilty that I hadn't visited in two years— maybe I would have noticed it if I had.

My mother asked us to bring her a special pillow from home, so my Dad and I drove back to their house that afternoon. When I walked in, Mitzi and Maggie started barking and yelping uncontrollably, distressed. The basket cross-stitch was still hanging in the spot where I last saw it, but I noticed that the familiar cigarette smell was commingling with something else that I couldn't quite pinpoint. The odor got stronger as I approached my mom's bedroom, which was oddly dark for a bright Florida day. I flipped on the light and gasped: all of her windows had been blacked out with black garbage bags, secured to the walls with duct tape. It looked like a scene from a scary movie, and just as I was about to unleash on my dad all the questions that were racing through my mind, I saw him shaking his head. His shoulders were slumped, his eyes downcast as he explained that my mother had been bedridden for three months.

"She fell out of her bed and fractured her shoulder," he said in a monotone voice, eyes still fixed to the floor.

That explained the bedpan and pee pads on the floor next to her bed.

"Dad, why didn't you take her to the hospital sooner?" I asked.

"Sutton, you know your mother. She refused to go," he replied, his eyes finally meeting mine.

My heart lurched. I understood that my father felt he had no choice but to take care of her, because he would have had to physically drag her, kicking and screaming, to the doctor. But I couldn't understand how he had done that for three months and never noticed the mass on her thigh. That felt like too painful a question to ask him, so I never did.

I didn't and don't blame my dad for any of it. He seemed so overwhelmed— and scared. I was upset that he had kept it from me, and that it had gotten so bad.

Eventually, he told me that my mom had admitted she had something on her leg but kept it bandaged and hidden from him. I knew he was wrestling with his own guilt, as I was wrestling with mine. What makes me incredibly sad is that if she had gone to the doctor right away, she might still be alive. Instead, she let that tumor grow for two years.

That night, I wound up getting a room at the Holiday Inn Express down the road so I could have space to process what was happening. The house was also filthy, which shocked me. My mom had always been a stickler for cleanliness. She was a germophobe who always used vinegar and water to clean, no chemicals, because she was scared they would make her sick. She was constantly vacuuming when I was a child or whenever I would come and visit. Seeing her ashtray overflowing with cigarette butts and ash, the visible tufts of dog hair balled up in the corner, not to mention the crumbs on the bedcovers and floor, made me realize how sick she really was.

Hunter arrived the next day. While they

had never hashed out their differences, I was so relieved that they were at least speaking to each other again.

Still, when he walked into her hospital room, she greeted him with an eyeroll and a sigh, followed by "Well, I guess I'm dying now."

We all laughed.

I was in such denial—it never occurred to me that this might kill her.

My brother and I weren't prepared for what the house looked like, and we immediately got to work. We spent that week together cleaning out her room. First, we removed the trash bags from the windows—the light pouring in only highlighted the filth that had accumulated in her room. Next, we stripped the bed, and that's when we realized how badly her mattress was soiled. We opened all the windows to air the place out, then called a professional company to come shampoo the carpets and do a deep clean of the entire house. During our deep clean, we discovered that she had fifty rolls of toilet paper in her bedroom closet and fifty bags of unopened Clinique bonus gift bags stored underneath her bathroom sink. She would always send my father to collect sample bags, but she never used them.

"She doesn't have any normal clothes," I said, as I pulled out the housecoats and robes that had filled her closet.

"She doesn't need any," Hunter replied. "She never leaves the house."

I picked up a giant, dark-aqua velour robe that would have swallowed her frail frame.

"Maybe this was how she hid the mass from Dad," I said.

"Mom, we're going to buy you a new mattress," I told her the next day at the hospital.

Her face screwed up so tight she could barely spit the words out. "You won't pick the right one. I'll hate it," she said, turning her head away from me and Hunter.

"Mom, you can't sleep on the one you have now," my brother said. "It's soiled. We have to buy you a new one. We'll pick out a good one, I promise."

She kept her head turned away from us.

"I won't sleep on it," she said through clenched teeth. "I'll sleep on the floor."

Now that I'm the mother of a four-year-old, I understand this behavior. She had zero control, and it was infuriating to her.

My dad stayed with her while Hunter and I went back and forth, cleaning the house and visiting them in the hospital. It was the first time the four of us had been together like that in over twenty years. We brought in fast food and watched the Weather Channel, my mom's favorite. (Odd for someone who never left her house.) My dad and I played Candy Crush, and Ted sent a bouquet of roses and daisies. When my mom read the card, she looked at me with her eyebrows raised and I saw the faintest hint of a smile. In between hospital visits, my brother and I played putt-putt at Gator Golf, and one night we made vodka ice cream floats and reminisced. I was so grateful he was there.

That week, my mother had surgery to remove the tumor, and it left a giant hole in her thigh. Hunter called it her "shark bite." My mom thought that was funny. We kept humming the theme from *Jaws*. They transferred her to a rehab facility a few days later. Hunter went back to New York, and I headed back to LA. I planned to come back in a week to help my dad and then go straight to New York, where I had a three-week concert run booked at the Café Carlyle. Hunter would come back down, and we would tag-team helping my dad take care of her.

It was a relief to be back in LA with Ted, but I was so distracted. I found it hard to think of anything other than my mother. I couldn't shake the fetid scent of her bedroom or the image of those black trash bags on her windows. Or wrap my head around how she would allow that tumor to get so big.

On August 15, Ted asked me to meet him for dinner at Musso and Frank, a very famous old-school restaurant on Hollywood Boulevard. It was chicken pot pie night.

"How are you doing?" he asked between bites of carrots and flaky pastry.

"I feel like I'm drowning," I replied.

After dinner, we walked across the street to the Egyptian Theatre to watch *The Lady Eve*, starring Barbara Stanwyck. I was so distracted that I didn't really enjoy the movie, but I didn't let on to Ted, who is a major movie buff and comes from Hollywood royalty. His maternal grandmother was Marian Nixon, a silent film actress who transitioned into the talkies. She was married to Ted's grandfather, William Seiter, a famous director who worked with Shirley Temple, the Marx brothers, and Ginger Rogers and Fred Astaire. Both had stars on the Hollywood Walk of Fame, and Ted suggested taking a stroll to visit Marian's, which was nearby. I agreed, but I was just going through the motions. Ted was talking about a movie he had recently seen, and the only thing I could focus on, other than my mother, were the blisters starting to form on my heels from my wedge sandals. At one point, I looked at him and noticed he was sweating.

"Are you okay?" I asked.

"It's hot!" he said, dabbing his forehead.

We turned right on Vine and walked a block until Ted realized that Marian's star was the other way. So we turned around and walked the other way until we were finally at her star.

"This is great!" I said.

It was—but my feet were now throbbing and it was ten at night in a sketchy area of Hollywood. I just wanted to go home.

Ted brought out a bottle of water, which he poured over the star, and napkins, which he used to clean it. The next thing I knew, he was down on one knee, looking up at me.

"What are you doing?" I said.

"Do you want to get married?" he said.

This was a complete surprise.

"What are you doing?" I repeated. I had heard him but wanted to make sure I understood what he was saying.

"I have a ring!" he said.

He pulled out a little worn leather pouch from his pocket, and inside was his great-grandmother Emily's ring.

I think I said, "Of course," but I was so caught off guard, and frankly, confused. I knew I wanted to marry him, but I was such an emotional wreck! All I could think as he tried to slip the tiny platinum-and-diamond heirloom on my finger was, *Why is he doing this now?*

I now realize why he wanted to propose at that difficult moment in my life: he wanted me to know he was there for me. I didn't have to hide anything from him. He loved me at my most vulnerable and scared.

Back home, we drank a bottle of wine by the pool. Ted was excited and giddy. I was still in shock. That night we called his mom, who knew he was proposing because she had given him the ring.

"Oh, this is spectacular! I'm so thrilled! Congratulations!" she said.

I was still processing everything that was happening with my parents and decided to wait to tell them. I did call Hunter. Ted and I had only been together for eight months, so he thought I was calling to say that we were moving in together. He was surprised when I said I was engaged.

"Well, congratulations!" he said.

He hadn't met Ted yet, but he knew I was crazy about him.

I waited a few days to tell my dad.

"Maybe let's wait and tell your mom when y'all get here," he said.

I knew he was too overwhelmed to take

it all in. To be honest, I was too. My dad sounded defeated. I understood, as did Ted, who told me that he wanted to be with me when I shared our news with my mother. A week later, we flew to Florida, with Linus, arriving in time for my mother's sixty-sixth birthday: August 26, 2013. She was still at the rehab center, healing from the surgery and learning how to use a walker. We brought her key lime pie, one of her favorites, and I showed up wearing the ring, which was so small it wound up on my pinky.

I was nervous. Ted, however, was not. He walked into that rehab, holding my hand, smiling.

My mom was in her wheelchair in the courtyard. It was hot and humid, the air speckled with those pesky no-see-um gnats, but she still seemed happy to see us. Ted was his usual charming and gentlemanly self.

"Hello, Ted," my mother said as he pulled a chair up to her wheelchair.

He got right down to business: "I know it's often better to ask forgiveness than permission, but I would love to marry your daughter."

Instead of answering right away, she looked at me and then slowly turned her eyes toward Ted. Then, with the flicker of a smile, she said, "We'll see."

My mom spent another week in the rehab center and kept saying how much she loved the food there, especially the chicken salad sandwiches and chocolate pudding. The steroids she was taking made her suddenly excited about food. We brought her pasta and pie and Dunkin' Donuts Munchkins, which she gobbled up. That was a positive sign, and yet she was having trouble forming sentences, her words slurring as the tumors in her brain impacted her speech.

She was going to start radiation treatments in an attempt to stop the cancer from spreading further. Other than housecoats, she had nothing to wear to those appointments, so she asked me to go shopping for her. On Ted's last day, he came to Macy's with me. I got so sad as I riffled through the racks of clothes looking for something she might like. I ended up buying a Brooks Brothers button-down dress with a belt and a yellow-striped cotton sundress—her favorite color, and mine. I selected things that reminded me of what she wore when I was a teenager, kind of like how she always had my dad buy me Frosted Flakes and Entenmann's cookies when I would come visit as an adult. We were all stuck in time, and it made me realize how little I knew about her—or if she even had a certain style.

Although I knew she had stage four melanoma, and that it was one of the deadliest cancers, I never once entertained the thought that she was dying. That was more than I could take in—after all the years of struggling to understand her, I finally had an opportunity to get to know my mom. It didn't make any sense, but I was hopeful for the future.

When I said goodbye to Ted at the airport, he gave me his gray cardigan so I'd have a piece of him with me. That sweater became my security blanket.

Then I drove back to the rehab center in Cape Canaveral in my big boat of a rental car with the Macy's bags in the front seat.

My mom's face lit up when I showed her what I had bought, especially that yellow sundress. That got the biggest smile.

"Thank you," she tried to say after I showed her all the outfits. The words tangled in her mouth.

"I hope you like what I picked out."

She nodded yes.

My mom was released from the rehab center, wearing her brand-new yellow dress. She wanted me to drive her back to the house in my big rental car because she hated my dad's little red Saturn. "It's a death trap," she had complained in the past.

We wheeled my mom to my giant Monte Carlo and I drove about 35 miles per hour with her in the front seat next to me. She looked so small and scared. After so many years of being afraid of her, I was starting to see a crack in her angry façade.

We got her settled in her room. She didn't mention the new mattress, but she did sleep on it that night. I bought a meal tray at Target so I could bring food to her room, and I even tried to recreate the rehab center's chicken salad that she'd loved so much. The day of her first radiation appointment coincided with a cabaret class I was supposed to teach via Skype for Ball State.

When I told my mother that I couldn't take her, I saw a flicker of fear in her eyes.

"Do you want me to come with you?" I asked.

She nodded yes, so I gave my regrets to my class.

I spent the next two weeks cooking, cleaning, and driving my mother to her radiation treatments in her new dresses. I kept Ted and Hunter abreast of what was happening, including that she had been cleared for a new experimental drug. There was hope on the horizon.

It couldn't come fast enough. Her ability to speak was declining rapidly, proof the tumors were interfering with those parts of her brain that targeted speech. She was still chain-smoking, and I begged one of the doctors to tell her to stop. He shrugged and shook his head. He knew it was no use. My mom would lie in bed with a box of donut holes and smoke. One day I went in and she was trying to light a pen. The next day she tried putting deodorant on her lips. That night she asked my dad to sleep on the floor by her bed. She was frightened, and so were we. It was so hard to witness this decline and feel so powerless. I knew that I needed to be there for her and for my dad, but I was overwhelmed.

I needed somewhere to place all the feelings whirling around inside me, and I decided to make another granny-square blanket. I found a pattern online that had an owl with sweet button eyes at the center of each square. Inspired, I drove out to Michaels to buy the yarn: turquoise, hot pink, hunter green, orange, white, gray, and black. Sitting on my parents' couch, with Linus by my side, I crocheted square after square of plump, big-eyed, whimsical birds. I have always loved owls, and there was something comforting and reassuring about making a series of them. Each one made me smile as it appeared, stitch by stitch. I particularly loved sewing on their little button eyes and weaving in all the ends of each square so they could double as woolen coasters. I decided to border each square in black—the only thing I've ever made that's black, perhaps in an unconscious nod to the mourning I was already beginning to feel.

A missing—of the mother I wanted and the mother I had—that was bigger than me at that moment.

I made twenty or so owl squares during my two-week stay. As I was packing to head back up to New York in early September for my Carlyle run, I put them all in a tote bag. We were still waiting for the experimental drugs to arrive, but by then, my mom had stopped talking entirely. When I asked her to write what she was trying to say, she just wrote scribbles. Her beautiful cursive penmanship was gone. I told her I was just going away for a few weeks, and that I would be back. I told her I would check in with Dad daily. I did not say, "You're going to be fine!" But that was my desperate hope.

Right before I left for the airport, I sat by her bed and took her frail hand in mine.

"I love you, Mom."

I felt her fingers squeeze mine.

She mumbled, "I love you, too."

I could barely make out the words, but they were there.

While I was in New York, Hunter and Jen went down to be with her, as did my

Aunt Mary Anne and my Uncle Johnny. She greeted her sister and brother the same way she'd initially treated me—so angry, refusing to see them by turning her head and shutting her eyes. That was all she had left.

Aunt Mary Anne told me that Johnny acquiesced, but she forced herself in the room, determined to reconcile. The Stubborn Sisters. By the end of that visit, Mary Anne said my mother patted the bed so her sister would sit next to her, friends once more.

I was keeping tabs with everyone throughout the day and performing at night. I love the Carlyle. The room seats about ninety people who are packed tight at elegant, dimly lit bistro tables that come right up to the stage. Michael Rafter and I had put together this show before I met Ted—Michael playing piano while I sang. My friends joked it was my "single and horny" show because the songs included "The Lies of Handsome Men" and an old trunk song called "I Want to Be Seduced." I did super fun and flirty renditions, which I particularly loved singing knowing Ted was in the audience.

It was a Saturday night, the end of my second week of a sold-out run. The first set went well, and I headed up to our hotel suite to rest before the second one. When I saw that I had a voicemail from my dad, all the fizzy adrenaline drained from my body.

"Sutton, your mom is back in the hospital." His voice sounded subdued. "They had to put her on life support."

Ted noticed my energy shift.

"Is everything okay?" he asked.

"It's my mom," I replied.

There was no time to process the enormity of this news. I had to go back downstairs and sing a seventy-minute set—and I was expecting friends from high school, some of whom knew my mom. Members of Ted's family were coming, too.

Ted put his arm around me as I called Hunter, who was back in New York, to let him know the news. I barely remember that conversation, only that I told my brother that I would fly to Florida the following day, knowing that he would, too.

Somehow, I made my way back to the stage and took my spot next to the piano.

I was going to sing the same set I had just finished. Easy. *Just sing, Sutton*, I thought. *You know how to do this.* I made my way through most of the songs without missing a beat. But my mind was racing. I needed to help my dad. I needed to see my mom. No one had said anything about the possibility of life support. What did that even mean? It was all happening too fast.

I had two songs left.

The next song was "Sunshine on My Shoulders." I flashed back to our wood-paneled living room in Augusta, Georgia, my mom smoking a cigarette and putting a tape of John Denver's greatest hits into our eight-track player. She loved that album, and that song in particular. I closed my eyes and thought of how she, an agoraphobe who lined her windows with black garbage bags, was losing a fight with a cancer fed by sunshine.

I got through that song and stayed strong through Sondheim's classic "Anyone Can Whistle," which I merged with "Being Alive" from *Company*. I thought back to sitting in the living room watching Patti LuPone take the stage at Carnegie Hall. My mom saying, "You can do that." That moment placing me on the very trajectory that got me to this small stage at the Carlyle.

That song radically changed for me in one evening. Songs can do that. When I sang it during the first set, it was about me and the men in my life. But when I sang it during the second set, knowing that my mom was dying, I realized that it had actually always been about her. And how I was scared that my own fears—of living, and loving—would turn me into her.

I looked out into the audience and saw Ted smiling at me.

I had one song to go, the encore. I thought I made it through what should have been the most difficult performance ever.

I looked over at Michael, sitting at the piano, waiting for my signal to start, but all I could think of was the last time I saw my mother. The last words she said to me.

I nodded at Michael, and he started the first chords to James Taylor's "You Can Close Your Eyes." I closed mine as I felt each verse erupt inside me like a salty wave, the tears I thought I had kept at bay now breaking through.

"I'm sorry," I said out loud, in front of the crowd.

But it was really meant for her.

The following day, Hunter met me at the airport and we flew down together. Ted stayed in New York and hosted the bachelorette party I had planned for Megan. She was engaged to be married on September 30, and I had organized tea and manicures at the Carlyle.

Hunter and I met our father in the hospital lobby. He seemed so tired.

We went to her room and she looked so peaceful, once again lying amid all those wires and beeping machines. But this time, a tube was attached to her mouth, forcing breath into her body, keeping her alive. My father explained that she had developed a cough and was having trouble breathing. This time, she agreed to be taken to the hospital. They admitted her, but while she was in her room, her eyes became fixed and she stopped breathing, so they had to intubate her.

That first night, Hunter and I slept at the house, and the next morning, we were back in the room with her when a doctor came in.

"Why is she still on life support?" he asked us gruffly. "What are we waiting for here?"

I stared at him in disbelief—and I'm still angry about that. He was so crass and unfeeling. I learned from another doctor, who was kind and patient, that my mom had pneumonia that wouldn't clear because the cancer had spread to her lungs. My brother and I had to tell my father in the horrible room with the vending machines that we had to take her off life support.

"We just have to clear up the pneumonia and then we can start the new medication," my dad argued.

"Dad, it's time," Hunter said.

"She's not going to get better," I said. "We have to let her go."

He broke down crying.

The only other time I had seen my dad cry was at his mother's funeral.

"I can't believe I'm crying about your mom," my dad finally said.

That broke my heart: they had been married for forty-seven years but had been so unhappy. I understood.

They took her off life support and moved her to a quiet floor.

Ted flew down after the bachelorette party and brought us Sonny's BBQ, which we ate in the horrible room with the vending machines. He went back to my parents' house, and my dad, Hunter, and I stayed with my mom. That night, I slept on the floor on pillows.

"How will we know?" I asked one of the nurses.

She said, "When it's time, you will see her veins go blue and her breathing will get shallow."

We were watching and waiting.

The next morning, her breath started slowing... and then she would breathe. And then ten seconds later she would breathe again. I held one hand, Hunter the other. My dad was touching her face when she stopped breathing again. This time, for good.

My dad kissed her forehead and said, "Have a nice flight."

Then he walked over and opened the blinds. He had read somewhere that a spirit needs light.

After my mom died, one of the nurses gave us a candle. I was touched, but then I noticed the glass container was cracked—that seemed symbolic.

Being in the room when my mom died, I felt an unmooring. Like one of the girls I drew throughout my twenties, I was plummeting through the air. When we arrived back at my parents' home, I collapsed crying in Ted's arms. He caught me. There was nothing to say. He just held me.

My dad grabbed a six-pack of Miller Lite from the refrigerator and said, "Let's go to the beach." He wanted to bring the dogs too.

I said, "Dad, you can't bring beer or dogs to the beach! It's not allowed."

He said, "Let them arrest me."

That night, we started talking about funeral arrangements and burial plots. We decided to have her funeral in Whiteville and bury her next to Dada, knowing she would've been mad about it but also realizing that we had no other options. She had no ties to anywhere except where she was born.

My mother died on September 26, 2013, at the age of sixty-six—just like her mother. Megan was getting married on September 30, and I was one of her bridesmaids. I flew back on the twenty-eighth, went to her wedding, and scheduled my mom's funeral for October 1. Ted and I flew to Whiteville, and Stephanie took three planes to fly across the country from Los Angeles so she could be there. When I stepped into the church, I saw Michael Rafter.

"What are you doing here?" I asked, surprised.

He just smiled and gave me a big hug.

All my mom's siblings were there as well—including Mary Anne, who had also gone to see my mother in her coffin the night before the funeral. She wanted to see her sister one last time.

Hunter gave the eulogy—and he did not hold back. He was honest. He admitted that she could be difficult and that she had perfected the ability to push people away.

He also said how grateful he was to be able to spend her final days with her.

"We were by her side as she left this world," he said. "She knew that she wasn't alone. We stood with her as a family. This family that she created and nurtured. And it was in that moment that I realized that nobody truly leaves us. They live on in our memories and in the stories we tell."

After the funeral, my dad rented a house in Myrtle Beach. Ted and I went to spend time with him there, as did Hunter and Jen. Stephanie came too. We played putt-putt and ate fried shrimp and went for beach walks and did puzzles. Stephanie found a sushi restaurant, and my dad tried sushi for the first time ever.

I saw a tiny spark in him.

I spent another week with him in October to help him deal with all of my mom's things. We went to Epcot, drinking and eating our way around the World Showcase pavilions. No better place than Disney World to escape reality!

My dad hadn't been out of the house much for so many years that he was a little shy at first. Like a captive coming out of his cave, blinking in the sun. One afternoon, he saw a neighbor and told her that his wife had died. She was shocked—she had no idea that he had been married.

As I write these memories, these stories of my mother, I keep coming back to those owl squares. They're still sitting in the same bag I put them in the last time I saw my mother alive. They sat in that bag for a year before I first attempted to piece them together. By then, I had started shooting *Younger*, the new TV series I was cast in after *Bunheads* wasn't picked up for a second season. I would sit in my chair between scenes and work on finishing all the little squares, sewing in the ends of each square, which is the last step before stitching the whole thing together. But I somehow couldn't finish it. And I still haven't.

The pieces themselves are so sweet, but they stayed in the bag, and I started to think of them as my mourning blanket. I hadn't put it together yet because I was still figuring out where all the pieces went.

Also, what would I do with it once it was finished? Would I give it to my daughter? When Emily was born, several years after my mom died, someone suggested I sew the squares together and give the blanket to her. I immediately dismissed the thought. "It has too much pain and sadness woven into it," I said. Then I thought of Hunter's eulogy, and how all we have left are the stories, and I realized how this blanket is the story of my daughter's grandmother. One I am still trying to tell.

CHARACTER PORTRAITS

The Thanksgiving after my mom died, my father drove to New York to spend the holiday with Hunter, Jen, Ted, and me in New York. That was the first time we were all together for any holiday in over twenty years.

That spark I saw in my father in Myrtle Beach was now a glowing ember.

I'd lost my mom, but I saw the possibility of getting my father back in the wake of my mother's death. The man who loved to plant marigolds, and barbecue burgers, and make tomato sandwiches. Oh, how I had missed him.

Hunter hosted the meal at his lake house,

not far from mine, and gave a toast: "I'm so happy that we're all together. And, Dad, we are all so happy that you're here." He was choking back tears.

My dad sat there, smiling. I could tell that he, too, wanted to make up for lost time. That trip was one of many reconnections that he made that fall. He went to North Carolina to see his sister Linda and his Uncle Ken, Paw Paw's brother, for the first time in decades. He also came to the opening night of *The Bridges of Madison County*, a brand-new musical that Hunter was in, which was the first time he ever saw his son on Broadway. That Christmas, Hunter called to say that Dad sent a holiday card addressed to both Hunter and Jen—the first ever. They had been together twenty years. He also made a four-day road trip in his little red Saturn to visit me in Los Angeles, his shih tzus, Mitzi and Maggie, riding shotgun. By then, Ted had sold his bachelor pad and moved in with me, and I was so excited about having my dad see my house and meet my friends that I decided to host a dinner party the night he arrived. Ted's mom, Jessica, came with her husband, Jay, as did my friend Megan and her husband, Adam. I made spaghetti and meatballs and realized, just as everyone was arriving, that there wasn't enough food for everyone.

It didn't matter. In the middle of dinner, my dad excused himself to go upstairs, claiming that he was worn out. But then he came back downstairs almost immediately, and announced, "I think I need to go to the hospital."

He was pale and trembling, and I thought he was having a heart attack. I tried to stay calm, but I felt the panic coursing through my body. I sprinted out the door to go get my car, which was parked down at the bottom of a hill to make room in the carport for our guests. I kept thinking as I ran, *This cannot be happening. Not him. Not now.*

Ted ushered my dad to the car, and Megan sat in the back seat with my father, who was now shaking uncontrollably. She started playing the alphabet game to calm him down. She'd say a letter and ask him to say a word that started with that letter. A: apples. B: basketball C: chocolate chip cookies.

We finally got him to the ER and learned that the shaking was due to dangerously high blood pressure. They gave him medication, but that experience was a precursor to the triple bypass he would have two years later. We drove back to the house, exhausted and relieved. The whole experience rattled me: Ted and I had started to think about having children, and that meant I was reimagining what my family could look like. Ted had lost his dad the year before I met him, and I had just lost my mom. The thought of losing my dad as well was too much.

The stressful start to his visit didn't diminish our time together. We went to Stephanie and David's, where he got to play with the twins—the "miracle babies" Stephanie had conceived via IVF the year before—and I saw the glimmer of the granddad he would become. We also went bowling at Pinz on Ventura, and to see *The Wolf of Wall Street*, which Ted had worked on (an incredibly racy movie to watch sandwiched between your father and fiancé, FYI!), followed by dinner at Musso and Frank. We even took him to Disneyland with Adam and Megan, and then got In-N-Out Burger on the way home. We packed it in!

After my dad left, Ted and I went on a short trip to Hawaii. His mother looked after Linus and Charlie, Ted's Labrador-chow mix, while we were gone. When we picked the dogs up, we noticed Linus was panting, so we took him to the vet. Eventually we learned, after many more visits and tests, that he had pulmonary fibrosis—and that there was no cure.

I was still shaky from my dad's incident at the ER, and this news reignited all of those panicky feelings. Linus had been my constant. He got me through the most painful periods of my life. He was always by my side—until then. He started to isolate himself, away from me, Ted, and Charlie. We'd be in the kitchen or living room, and I'd find him curled up on the bed alone. I could tell he was in pain. He was my responsibility, and I felt like I was letting him down. We did everything we could to prolong his life, but on February 22, Ted texted me to say, "I think Linus has had his last good day." The doctor had warned us that he would decline quickly.

We were in Manhattan by then, as I was shooting the pilot of *Younger*. As soon as I got home from the set, Ted and I took Linus to the Animal Medical Center in Midtown. The fibrosis had gotten so bad that he was gasping for air. It was too much to see this sweet bundle working so hard. We decided to put him down that same evening. Ted and I were both in the room. Linus gave me one final kiss on the nose before the vet gave him the injection. As I watched his little body go limp, I felt like my heart had been ripped in two. I immediately regretted the decision. All the love and pain I'd felt about losing my mother was finally unleashed—I cried harder over Linus than I had when my mother died.

I understand why: dogs love you unconditionally. There are no strings. No baggage. There's just love. He taught me how to care for something other than myself, and he became the receptacle for all the grief I felt. Ted and I both believed that he knew he could go because I had found Ted. The night Linus died, Ted was curled up on the couch crying.

"God damn it," he said. "Linus made me love him!"

Linus had that effect on people.

Losing my mother, followed by losing Linus, made me realize that I had some serious healing to do. I had only just begun to see the light my mother had inside of her shortly before she died. I had seen that flicker in my father—and panicked when I thought I might lose him too. And I had met Ted and seen the possibility of building a new family with him. There was so much to process.

The summer before my mother died, I did a one-night-only concert of the musical *Violet* as part of City Center's Encores! Off-Center series. Michael Rafter was the one who introduced the show to me— his ex-wife Jeanine Tesori had composed the music for it pre-*Millie*. It was her first musical and so magnificent.

Violet is about a young woman from North Carolina traveling by bus to see a preacher in Tennessee. She has a deep scar that slashes across her face, starting at her eyebrow, running along the bridge of her nose, and continuing down her cheek. We learn through the course of the musical that her father accidentally struck her with an ax blade when she was young. The scar has defined Violet. It is who she thinks she is, how she thinks the world sees her. She believes that the preacher will remove her scar, and so heal her. That he has the power to make her not only be beautiful but also feel beautiful.

The evening was so well-received that the Roundabout Theatre Company decided to mount the production on Broadway with me as Violet.

When I look back at the roles I've played, I'm astonished at how they've tracked with my own evolution. I was Millie, that wide-eyed optimist. And I still make jokes about playing Fiona, the ogre princess, during such a painful period of my life. Reno was about finding my own inner core and strength. Violet was about forgiveness and accepting one's self, scars and all.

I realized, in preparing for this role, that there are scars you see and scars you don't. Some heal and others remain big open wounds. Some you forget about and some you wear like a mark of victory, or of shame. Violet's scar was obvious; mine was not.

I was so struck by the parallels between these four characters that I made a series of sketches. None of them had facial features—no eyes or mouths. You could tell Millie by her bobbed hair and Reno by her platinum coif, while Fiona wore a crown and Violet had a jagged scar running across her face. I hung the four portraits in my dressing room. Millie, Fiona, and Reno were reminders of where I had been— Violet was where I was headed. In the play, Violet goes on a journey to be healed. I was on a similar journey.

We began rehearsals in February 2014. Leigh Silverman was the director. She knew that I had just lost my mom and that I was still in a lot of pain processing that relationship. Leigh somehow understood that the shiny, people-pleasing veneer that had been my armor for so many years was now unavailable to me. My mother's death unmoored me. And in that break, there was an opening. Something profound was happening. It was almost as if someone had taken down the blackout shades within me, and the light pouring in was both stunning and blinding. I was scared, and compelled to move toward it. Leigh pushed me to go there, to trust myself and not be afraid of the feeling that might arise as I approached it. Playing this scarred woman in search of something to make sense of her pain gave me a path toward my own healing. Along the way, I was forced to access parts of myself that I hadn't before: the broken, the ugly, the angry, the unseen.

Violet was an unbelievable gift. In every single performance, I excavated another layer of the pain and sadness and darkness I had been holding inside for thirty-eight years. I mourned my mom. Not only her death but the loss of a mother I didn't have for so many years.

I forgave her.

I accepted her.

That was my journey. My father had his own. He came to the opening night of *Violet*—it was his first time seeing me on Broadway since *Millie*. When he came backstage afterward, his eyes were still misty. "That last song really got me," he said.

It's called "Bring Me to Light."

Not long after, he told me that he had put up a profile on Match.com and had gone on a couple of dates. He also decided to get his teeth fixed. He hadn't been to the dentist in probably fifteen years, and many of his teeth were badly broken off and stained from so many years of coffee and cigarettes. As a result, he mumbled when he talked and never smiled, in an attempt to hide his teeth.

When he said he wanted to have them done in time for my wedding, I took that as a sign. He was also thinking about selling the house. My father was reinventing himself and reclaiming his life.

I understood—because I was doing the same.

Ted and I got married October 25, 2014, outside in the garden at the San Ysidro Ranch in Montecito. I wanted a small wedding—Ted and I made sure we had enjoyed at least one dinner with every guest who was invited. That was more important to me than my dress or shoes.

Ted's mom and brother walked him down the aisle. Megan walked with our four-legged flower girl Mabel, the sweet pup we adopted after Linus died. And then I followed between my brother and dad. We lined the aisle with pots of yellow roses— my mom's favorite flower, and mine, too. They are now planted in our garden in Los Angeles. And we had lots of photos taken! They're all over our house, on display. In all of them, we are smiling big toothy smiles— including my sweet dad.

PRAYERS TO THE FERTILITY GODS IN COPIC MARKERS

I was feeling cautiously optimistic as I sat down at my long wooden kitchen table and pulled out supplies to make a new drawing: a fresh pad of paper and a pencil, an eraser, a bin of colored Sharpies, and another bin of Copic markers, which have paintbrush tips. After a year and a half of trying to get pregnant and not succeeding, Ted and I decided to pursue fertility treatments. I had just done the "ovary stimulation" part of the process, and it worked. Always the overachiever, my body produced not two or six but fifteen eggs, which were still in my body as I sat and started to draw.

I pulled out a dark-green fine-tip Sharpie and drew fifteen little circles.

Fifteen little chances.

Fifteen little opportunities.

Every circle I drew was a tiny meditation.

Please let all the needles and the hormones be worth it.

I drew another circle.

How will it feel to be pregnant?

Another one.

Am I ready to be a mother?

A small cluster formed.

I wonder if it'll be a boy or a girl.

I put my pen down.

What the fuck am I doing?

With each circle came another question. Another wish. Another dream. And with each tiny bubble that emerged, I felt more certain. I would become a mother. I was on my way.

It was mid-May, and I was making this drawing for an art show called "Side by Side" that I was doing with my old friend and dresser Julien Havard at the Hamilton-Selway gallery in Hollywood. In addition to showing our own individual work, Julien and I were also going to collaborate on several pieces, combining his swirly style with my interconnected-circle approach, a playful take on pointillism. The opening was in June, which meant I had less than five weeks to prepare for it.

It was my sixth show with Julien. In the past, I had done drawings of animals, or flowers, or those girls with flowing hair. I did a series of Broadway character portraits— Violet, Millie, Reno, and Fiona—the year before, in what was my first LA art opening, followed by another exhibition in Province-town that focused entirely on dogs. Right before my mom died, I'd showed the giant word collages BADASS and YOU ROCK, as well as two others I had done (YOU ARE LOVED and NO FEAR) at a Manhattan gallery.

The work always reflected something personal that was happening in my life at that moment: for this show, I decided to focus on fertility. I wanted to make a series that would allow me to meditate on what was happening at that moment in my body. This felt so much bigger than me. In the past, I was able to work extra hard to make things happen. But at this moment, I felt

I had to embrace the concept of higher powers. My relationship with religion had morphed over the years—I had become more spiritual than churchgoing religious, and I wanted to conjure all the deities to help guide me on this particular quest. So I decided to make pictures of fertility gods.

The first one I drew was Atabey, the supreme goddess and Mother Earth figure of the Taíno people indigenous to the Caribbean, who is worshiped as a deity of fertility, childbirth, and fresh water, among other things. One of the most popular images of her depicts her squatting, her belly big between her bent knees, her arms raised, a hand next to each ear. The story goes that she gave birth to her sons without actually having sex. (Going through IUI and all it entails, I related!) I began by filling the page with small, orange-rimmed circles that I colored in with shades of lime green, lemon yellow, pale pink, and sky blue. Over time, the corner started to look as if it had been sprinkled with confetti made up of little jewel-like drops. A celebration. A new life.

Next, I outlined Atabey in a pale lime green. Her body was made up of more interlaced bubbles, but these I filled in dark purple, deep blue, and brick red, with hints of cinnamon brown scattered throughout. My style of drawing worked well for Atabey. The interconnected bubbles that I had used in so many other drawings leading up to this one made it look as if her ovaries were teeming with eggs, like mine were at that very moment.

As I worked my way through the drawing, I thought, *Make me fertile. Make me willing to receive.*

It felt strange, to suddenly want to become a mother so badly. For most of my life, my career had been my focus. Plus, my mom had made a prediction when I was in my early twenties that now haunted me. "Sutton, you won't have children," she said. "Hunter will." I don't recall why she said that, only that it stung. Back then, motherhood was the furthest thing from my mind. At the time, I wasn't even sure that I wanted to be a mom. Still, her comment confused me. What did she see in me that made her

say such a thing? Maybe I was too career focused and didn't have the "motherly" gene.
As I got older and saw friends starting their
families, I began to worry—what if she was
right? It all felt beyond my reach.

I know now that I was still finding myself.
And that I needed to do that in order to
find the right partner, which was important
to me in order to start a family. As independent as I was, I didn't want to do that
alone. Funnily enough, Hunter and Jen
never had kids. And now that I had found
Ted, I was finally ready. When I broached
the subject to Ted, he said, "Let's do it!"

At first, we just stopped using protection.
We were both *so* excited. It was all we could
think or talk about. We started talking about
baby names and where we'd want to raise
our child—New York? Los Angeles? We had
just bought a new apartment in Manhattan,
as we were spending more time there, and
the thought of raising a city kid was appealing. The culture, the experiences! But
Ted's family was in Los Angeles, where life
felt easier. We'd have more space! And did
I mention the sunshine? We never settled

on one or the other. Instead, I let my imagination run wild with all the possibilities—the places we would go together as a family, the blankets I would crochet for our kid. Imagining Ted wearing a Baby Bjorn on weekend hikes made me fall even more in love with him—and I couldn't wait to start painting murals on the nursery walls! These were new, thrilling thoughts. After so many years of preventing pregnancy, I was suddenly eager to become a mother!

The first time I got my period, I felt like such a failure. I thought it would be so easy! As the months rolled by, however, that feeling—that this was not going according to plan, that something was getting in the way—started to irk me. I continued to be shocked each month it didn't work. And then I began to wonder: Was my mother's prediction a premonition? I swatted that idea from my mind. I had a pretty good track record of making things happen through hard work. I was *determined.*

After a few months of just kind of winging it, I Googled "How to get pregnant at 38" and I learned that I was a "geriatric mother" and that the odds were slim. Like, 29 percent chances. I felt a pit in my stomach, a gnawing. I had heard about age-related fertility, but I thought it was bullshit or, at the very least, that it didn't pertain to me. Sure, I was thirty-eight, but my grandmother Lenora had my mother at forty-one and my uncle at forty-four. And my Aunt Mary Anne had my cousin Jayme at age forty-five! My friend Stephanie was thirty-nine when she first started trying to get pregnant—she was in LA and I was in New York at the time, but I remembered her telling me about taking her temperature throughout the day and making detailed flow charts. It felt so ridiculous to me then—until I learned that my ovaries were literally shriveling up. I decided to focus all my energy on getting pregnant, like Stephanie had.

I can do this, I thought as I downloaded an ovulation tracker app, made a flow chart, and bought a thermometer. Trying to get pregnant shifted from being a giddy, fun activity to being a crash course on windows of peak fertility. And once I found the hour each month when everything lined up, Ted and I both had to be game—or at least in the same state. That wasn't so easy when I was filming crazy hours with *Younger* and traveling for concerts most weekends, and Ted was finalizing a major script.

After another several months of failed attempts, my gynecologist did a few routine tests, which all came back normal. "Just keep trying," she said. "Give it another six months, and then we can start talking about other options."

Cut to a year and a half later: I was forty-one in May of 2016, and we decided to finally pursue fertility treatment.

I had some idea of what to expect from Stephanie; that was how she gave birth to Sophia and Orlando. After the flow charts didn't work, she went through four rounds of IUI (intrauterine insemination, where your eggs are stimulated but not extracted), which is much less invasive than IVF (in vitro fertilization, where they extract your eggs, fertilize them, and then put them in your uterus). At the time, it all sounded so very foreign and sci-fi to me, but I fully respected her choices. When IUI didn't work, she did a round of IVF, which ended in an ectopic pregnancy. Another round resulted in my godchildren being born. They are proof that IVF works.

Stephanie and I are a lot alike. When we set our mind on something, we make it happen. I knew how harrowing this road was—but I also knew it worked.

One of Ted's best friends from grade school is a doctor, and he recommended a fertility clinic in Pasadena. We made the appointment and drove out to the clinic, leaving enough time to stop at Pie 'N Burger, one of his favorite dive diners. Ted wanted to take me there because he used to go as a kid with his mom, and he thought that pancakes and eggs would add levity to a daunting day. Ted didn't really know anything about IVF beyond the fact that we had friends for whom it worked. We excitedly talked about our new adventure between bites of breakfast.

It was so much fun to imagine the kid we would have together. Ted's mom told me that when Ted was born, he had six fingers and toes on each hand and foot. They were removed when he was a baby, but Ted joked he was a new species of superhuman. I thought, *What if our baby has extra digits, too?* Ted is six foot four and I'm five foot nine—maybe our kid would be a basketball player! Extra digits could help them really grip the ball! We just kept daydreaming about who we would create together, and how someday we'd bring them back to Pie 'N Burger for pancakes and tell them about the role this place played in their origin story.

At the clinic, we waited in the lobby with the other hopeful couples. The giddiness I had felt at the diner began to dissipate as Ted and I sat in the silent waiting room. No one swapped stories or even made eye contact, despite the obvious fact that we were all there for the same reason. It was eerie. I then spotted the small sign stating that children weren't allowed in the waiting area, and I realized why: for those of us who did not yet have kids, seeing them, at this tenuous moment, could be too painful. I was now part of this strange club. For someone who had been so ambivalent about having children, I was surprised by what I was willing to do to become a mother.

Considering how vulnerable I was feeling, I expected our doctor to be warm and encouraging. So I was incredibly disappointed to meet this very matter-of-fact, almost blasé middle-aged man who seemed better suited to be a bank teller than a fertility doctor. All I wanted was someone to hold my hand through the whole ordeal, and he was just static. I dubbed him Dr. Personality.

"Let's take a look at what's going on in there," he said.

Next thing I knew, he was using a thinga-mabob that went up my hoo-ha, and that is as revealing as I'm going to get. I will say the experience deflated all that earlier excitement I was feeling. Buzzkill. As I lay on the table, I had to stay focused on the end goal. If this was what it took to get pregnant, then I was willing to do it. It didn't help that the doctor was so aloof. He didn't really talk me through anything or even look at me. He was focused on the computer screen, which was displaying fuzzy, granulated images of— my uterus? Ovaries? I had no idea.

"How are things looking?" I asked, in an attempt to break the excruciating silence.

"You're forty-one," he said, his eyes still fixed on the computer screen. "We should do IVF. And genetically test the embryos."

I was lying on the table, thinking, *Slow down, Dr. P!* What was he talking about? What were all those tiny dots on a screen? Was he seeing defects?

It was outrageous to me that a male fertility doctor who sees women at their most emotionally fragile states could be so detached and cold. I found the experience crushing.

Back in his office, he explained that my ovaries were still producing eggs, but because of my age, they could have genetic deformities. The only way to know was by retrieving them, inseminating them in a petri dish, and then genetically testing them before putting them back into my body. Ted was sitting next to me, holding my hand. We were both trying to absorb all this information, but I realized, at that very moment, that all the pressure and responsibility of bringing a child into this world fell to me. I was the one who was going to have to take the hormones, to stimulate my eggs, to go through the retrieval process. It felt like too much. I told the doctor that I wanted to start with IUI—at least my eggs would stay in my body for the insemination process. At least I could feel as if I had some control.

He replied, "You're wasting your time. You should go straight to IVF."

I wanted to punch him.

Instead, I took a deep breath and said, "I'd like to try IUI first." In my mind, I was thinking, *How dare you tell me what I can or can't do! This is* MY *body.*

"Ultimately, it's your choice," he said reluctantly.

For that process, I would need to take hormones to increase my egg production, and Ted would have to ejaculate into a cup so his sperm could be surgically inserted into me. The doctor used more scientific language, but that was how I interpreted it.

Super sexy, right?

We went home with pills I had to take daily, a bunch of tiny syringes, and a red plastic container for all the used needles. Those fun and thrilling nights of candlelight and lacy lingerie shifted to Ted injecting me in the belly every night for two weeks. This wasn't exactly how I imagined becoming a mother, but we tried to make it light and funny. Each dose was exciting and hopeful. We were getting one step closer to having a family.

When we went back to the clinic, Dr. Personality did an ultrasound and discovered that I had produced fifteen eggs! I felt oddly proud. We were one step closer. But I paid a high price for being an overachiever: the doctor still suggested we do IVF. If we continued with IUI, he cautioned, we could end up with multiples—not twins but quintuplets or more.

I immediately thought, *Octomom!* Followed by, *Hell no!*

We decided to move ahead with the IVF and made the appointment for the retrieval a few days later. In between, I sat down to draw Atabey. I was determined to do everything in my power to make this pregnancy happen, despite my late start—and that included taking hormones and summoning deities. I would prove my mom wrong: I could and would become a mother.

I finished that drawing and then went back to the clinic a couple days later for the retrieval. After being (thankfully) knocked out, I woke up in a curtained-off recovery room, and overheard the nurse delivering results to other patients through the thin material that separated one hopeful mother from another.

"We retrieved eight eggs," she said to one, who burst into happy tears.

"We were only able to retrieve two eggs," she said to another.

Silence.

When the nurse opened up my curtain, she was smiling. "We were able to retrieve all fifteen eggs," she said. "This is good news!"

My heart swelled up. My "geriatric" ovaries were still working!

The fertilization process was that same day. While I was getting the eggs removed, Ted was in his own private room. The doctor then "introduced" his sperm to my eggs in a lab. Hopefully they lit candles and played Barry White.

Now it was a waiting game. Over the next three or four days we would know if the fertilization process had worked. The goal was that the eggs would become embryos and our doctor would select the healthiest one to implant. In the end, eleven were fertilized and four were "top-notch" embryos; they get graded by how they look and how many cells have divided. The doctor said that they looked good but he still wanted them tested for abnormalities. Ted and I were ridiculously happy—it had worked!

Getting pregnant in late May would mean I could film the next season of *Younger* and be able to hide a swollen stomach. I was also booked to start rehearsals for an off-Broadway run of *Sweet Charity* at the New Group in October. According to my math, I would be five months pregnant by then, so that might be trickier. But I thought a baby bump might even add a layer to the character: Charity was a dance hall hostess. It could be interesting! I knew it was a stretch, but women work pregnant all the time. And besides, I would have a break after that. I could give birth in January or February and be back on set for season four of *Younger* if it was picked up again. It was all working out according to my plan.

Until the doctor suggested I take a month's rest. He said my uterus wasn't ready to receive the embryo. The hormones I had taken to produce these eggs had wreaked havoc on my uterine lining—it wasn't in the right shape to sustain implantation. *What? No, no, no, no!* That was not part of my plan! I couldn't wait a month. I was supposed to be back in New York to start filming in June. My window was right *now*.

That same day, Megan texted me a photo of her pregnancy test with the two pink lines.

We had talked about being pregnant at the same time, two giddy best girlfriends. She and Adam had started trying that month, and she got pregnant on her first try.

I had kept her up to date on my own trials and tribulations. She knew that we were getting ready for the implantation—but not the latest news.

"Wanna do this together?" she texted.

I started to cry. I was so happy for her and didn't wish infertility on anyone, but I was also envious.

"I think we should go ahead with the transfer," I said to Ted in the car after hearing from the doctor about my unstable uterus.

"Why?" he asked.

"I can't fly back while I'm filming. If we don't do it now, we'll have to wait. Megan is pregnant. We can go through it together. I feel like this is the time."

Against the doctor's guidance, we decided to do the transfer. We were just going to transfer one embryo and have the other three genetically tested. We drove to Pasadena at five a.m. on a Saturday at the end of May, and in a dimly lit room, a tiny invisible embryo was implanted inside of me. Dr. P printed an ultrasound photo with the tiniest prick of light. That was our little miracle. We hung it on our refrigerator.

Another waiting—and praying—period.

I used that time to focus on the remaining drawings I wanted to do for the art show with Julien. Drawing Atabey had grounded me, so I thought a few more fertility gods, goddesses, and deities couldn't hurt.

Next on the list was Kokopelli, a fertility god from the American Southwest. I was thrilled that he was a musical, flute-playing, dancing deity—it felt like a sign. As I drew him, using small circles in eggplant purples and sky blues, I thought about our wedding song, "The Folks Who Live on the Hill": "Someday we may be adding a wing or two, a thing or two." I imagined Kokopelli playing the song on his flute, dancing, against a sunset background in shades of bubblegum pink, pale orange, and tangerine, the crest on his head waving in the wind like bendy exclamation points. I also read that he brought good fortune to anyone who would listen to his songs, so my mantra, while I colored in all those tiny, interconnected dots was: "I am listening. Play your song." With each new drawing, I envisioned a little miracle growing inside of me.

The Manaia was next. I first saw this Māori symbol on a trip that Ted and I took to New Zealand earlier that year. Though different tribes have their own versions of the Manaia, the one we saw was depicted with the head of a bird, the body of a man, and the tail of a fish to represent the balance between sky, earth, and sea. It's a guardian talisman, a spiritual guide. My mantra for this one was: "Guide me. Keep me centered. Show me the way."

These drawings helped me see how badly I needed balance and guidance. I was doing this without a role model or teacher. Without a mother figure whom I could trust to show me the way. The universe was trying to tell me something—there was a reason I had waited this long. But there were still obstacles that I needed to remove.

The fourth and final drawing I did for this show was Ganesh, the Hindu deity who looks like a pot-bellied elephant, often shown sitting in the lotus position. Though not directly a fertility god, Ganesh is known as the "remover of obstacles," and I kept thinking something was getting in the way for me. Obstacles are real and tangible, but they are also emotional. I couldn't help but think my body was responding to a psychological fear that I would give birth to my mother—that her genes would be passed through me to my child. Or that I would become the mother she was to me. Those thoughts paralyzed me. Ganesh was also the god of new beginnings: I was ready for that.

Please clear the path for me, I thought to myself as I drew Ganesh, a symphony of purples and blues outlined in a brilliant gold. *Please let this work.*

I decided to do one last drawing—not for the show, but to hang in the "miracle" baby's room. Loosely modeled on the totem poles made by Indigenous artists in the Pacific Northwest, it shows five animal heads stacked one above the another, each representing someone who has supported me. Not the family I was born into, but the one I created. Stephanie is an elephant, loyal and family focused. I drew her first, as the base, because she was the sturdiest of us all. She also gave me the courage and inspiration to be a mom. Julien was next, and I made him a black cat, as he had two of them,

Honey and Sammy. Julien, like Stephanie, is adopted, and has been my constant since we first met. He has seen me at my best and my worst. Whether I'm winning a Tony Award or naked and crying on a dressing room floor, he loved me anyway. Megan is the penguin in the middle. Her nickname is "Menguin" (her middle name is Gwynn), which is fitting, because she loves those sweet waddling creatures (and her grandmother collected figurines of them). We played sisters on Broadway and became them in real life. She represented unconditional love and support in all things. Ted was next, the first man to make me want to be a mom and to help me understand the meaning of family. He is the puppy dog, lovable and loyal, holding me. And I am an owl on the top of the stack, wide-eyed, my wings outstretched, ready to fly.

I framed this picture and put it in our living room, a reminder that I did have a family to offer this child. *Someday*, I thought, *this will be in the baby's nursery.* Hopefully soon.

Right before the art opening, I was

scheduled to do a concert with the Boston Pops. Megan was joining me to sing our duet: "Flight," by Craig Carnelia. It would be my first time seeing her since she had become pregnant. I was anxious to talk to her about all the things she was feeling, and eager to know how her body was changing. My doctor told me to wait a few weeks before taking a pregnancy test to confirm the embryo had taken, but my breasts felt tender, my belly tingly. I couldn't stand the anticipation. Right before the concert, I took a pregnancy test. Sure enough, a faint second line appeared.

I called Ted, who was back in LA, in tears.

"I think I'm pregnant!" I said.

"*What?*" he said.

I was shaking and elated and relieved. The gods had answered our prayers!

I sent him a photo of the faint result and knew he received it when I heard him burst out laughing.

"All right!" he said.

That same day, I told Megan, and we both hugged each other hard. We were doing it, together, just as we had hoped and planned. That night, onstage, Megan and I glanced at each other, smiling. Two best friends, both pregnant, standing before a seventy-five-person orchestra. As we sang, "Wish me on my way," the violins, cellos, and French horns elevated our voices to new heights. We have sung that song together so many times, but this time, it felt different, even more beautiful and inspiring and hopeful. "And I will start to soar!"

This was the new beginning. My prayers were answered.

A few days later, I was flying back to LA for the art show when I felt the tiniest twinge in my gut. A cramp. *It could be gas*, I thought. But then I also noticed that my boobs were not as tender. Something had shifted, and all the excited anticipation I had felt drained out of my body. Back in LA, I did another pregnancy test. That second line was there but fainter.

Oh no, I thought. *This can't be.*

When I finally went to the doctor, he told me that the pregnancy was not viable.

I was heartbroken. Gutted. And mad at myself for not listening to him. He had been right. I should have waited. I was also mad at myself for thinking that I had any control over this, that I was so naïve as to think I could squeeze this major life moment into my work schedule.

The art show was the following week, on June 7. No one except Julien knew what Ted and I had been through. Friends from Los Angeles came to the opening, as did several of the *Younger* writers, and Darren Star, the show's creator. He even bought one of my pieces, which should have been thrilling. I put on a brave face and talked to people about my artwork with a forced smile, but inside, I felt so hollow. All the fertility drawings I had made were hanging on the walls, mocking me. Taunting me. "You thought you could just conjure us and make it happen. But it doesn't work that way. You'll see."

I got through that evening (barely) and had to regroup. That was our first attempt—Stephanie had gone through many! She was my cheerleader and reminded me that all hope wasn't lost: "My first implantation didn't take, but Sophia and Orlando came from the other embryos that I had from my egg retrieval. You still have three chances!"

I felt encouraged. We would wait a month. I could fly back on a weekend from filming and do another implantation. Everything was going to be okay.

A few days later, I was walking around a Sports Authority with Ted, when I got a call from the nurse, who said, "The embryos we tested all came back abnormal."

"What?" I said in disbelief. It felt like a fucked-up joke.

"I'm so sorry," she said.

If we wanted to try again, we'd have to start from scratch.

That was when the bottom fell out from beneath my feet.

I was going to start filming *Younger* later that month, and the season would take me right up to *Sweet Charity* rehearsals in October. I knew that would be grueling—not just the rehearsals, and learning an entire show, but the eight live performances a week! I didn't know if I could handle going through IVF at the same time. Fitting in more fertility appointments and egg transfers felt impossible. Plus, I was forty-one, and I knew that I didn't have much time left. I called Joe, my agent, to say, "I can't do *Sweet Charity*! It's too much."

He let me rant about all the reasons I had to bow out and then very quietly said, "Um, the entire show is built around you."

I was Charity Hope Valentine. One of my dream roles. An eternal optimist who just wants to be loved. Cy Coleman wrote the music for this beloved musical, and his estate's lawyer had specifically requested me to play the role. Leigh Silverman was directing.

I decided to take a breath and regroup. Make a new plan. I felt conflicted. Maybe I should just put my foot down and cancel everything so I could focus completely on getting pregnant. Instead, I had to psych myself up. "I will make this happen" once again became my mantra. "I will become a mother."

I could sense the gods watching me.

Since Ted and I were heading back to New York, we decided to try a new clinic and doctor. My gynecologist recommended

Dr. Janelle Luk, who reportedly was able to get viable eggs using fewer hormones. This was appealing, as I still felt tired and worn out from the first attempt and wasn't sure I could go through that process again while working. My schedule was even more intense than usual: I had also prearranged a weeklong hiatus from *Younger* to do a series of concerts in Japan that August.

Meanwhile, I learned that Liza, my character on *Younger*, was going to have a pregnancy scare this season. So at work I was playing a forty-year-old who had a college-aged child and feared getting pregnant that late in her life. And in real life, I was a forty-one-year-old desperately making up for lost time by praying to any and all gods and doing hormone injections in the hopes of getting pregnant. It was a mindfuck.

That summer, I'd come home exhausted after filming fourteen- to sixteen-hour days and still have to shoot hormones into my belly before bed. I squeezed in doctor appointments on the weekends. Dr. Luk was incredibly warm and relatable—realistic about my age but still optimistic. We felt so easy around her that we started making Star Wars jokes: "Use the force, Luk!"

Since you can't predict when your eggs will be ready, I had to tell the first assistant directors, who handle the schedule, "On the downlow, I'm not sure when, but I'll have to take a morning off for egg retrieval."

I thought the gods were listening when that procedure was set for a Saturday. That morning, Dr. Luk retrieved ten eggs. (Prolific once again!) That afternoon, I had a photo shoot for *Cosmopolitan* magazine featuring the *Younger* cast. When I arrived, I told Peter Hermann, my love interest on the show, "They got ten eggs!" He was the only cast member I shared my journey with. I knew that he and his wife, Mariska Hargitay, had their first child via IVF and then adopted their next two children. Peter was thrilled and said, "That is *great* news!"

Once again, I allowed myself to be hopeful. Maybe, just maybe, this time, it would work.

A few days later, we found out that four eggs were "top-notch" embryos, and a week later, Dr. Luk recommended that we implant two in order to increase our odds. I was hesitant at first. But then I thought, *This is how people have families!* Stephanie did it—so could I! After the disappointment of the first procedure, Ted and I were also willing to double our chances. The morning of the implantation, a transpo van waited outside the clinic to drive me back to the set to film three scenes. Dr. Luk didn't know I was heading straight to work—she had advised that I rest afterward, but my crazy work schedule would not allow that. I kept it all a secret and felt hopeful as I sat in the makeup chair, smiling to myself. I could do this.

Five days later, Ted and I boarded a thirteen-hour flight to Japan. I was nervous but Dr. Luk said travel was fine as long as I rested as much as possible. I had four concerts booked with my go-to guys: Michael Rafter on piano, Leo Huppert on bass, and Kevin Kuhn on guitar. The first show was in Osaka, followed by one in Yokohama and the last two in Tokyo. We had done the set many times, so that part was easy, but I was taking hormones daily in a different time zone. Ted and I scaled back our daily excursions so I could save energy for the evening concerts.

During the shows in Osaka and Yokohama, my belly was fluttery and my boobs hurt even more than they had before. I kept flashing Ted, asking, "Do they look different?"

"They look big," he'd respond. "Maybe a little veiny?"

I took these as good signs.

Our final stop was Tokyo. Japanese audiences generally were not as effusive as American crowds, so I was touched when I got a standing ovation at the end of that show. Afterward, a local theater group showed up backstage dressed as my various characters—Millie, Reno, Fiona, and Violet—and sang the sweetest version of the title song from *Thoroughly Modern Millie* for me. It was all so moving.

I was also relieved: one show to go.

That next day, Ted and I walked through Harajuku, an area of Tokyo known for its colorful street art and vintage stores. I got a tower of rainbow cotton candy. It was fun, but also such a hot and humid day that Ted sweated through his pants—he looked like he had just taken a shower fully dressed. Back at the hotel, I started to feel a little off. I kept telling myself it was the heat.

That evening, Ted walked me to the theater.

"Have a great show," he said.

As I was applying my makeup in the dressing room, I felt the strangest sensation. A pointed jab, as if someone had pricked me with a needle in my abdomen, followed by a ripple throughout my body, the slightest deflation. *It's not working*, I thought, fighting back tears.

The show was a blur. I was so grateful that I had sung all those songs dozens of times before, and that I knew how to sing through painful emotions, because the only thing on my mind was that something was preventing me from getting pregnant.

Back at the hotel, I was distraught. I did the at-home test I had brought with me in the bathroom, even though I already knew what the results would be. Ted waited in the living room of our suite. When I exited the bathroom, I just shook my head.

He hugged me, but I didn't feel it. I couldn't feel anything. I was numb.

That night, we went to have dinner at the hotel's revolving rooftop restaurant.

We were surrounded by panoramic views of Tokyo's skyline, but I felt claustrophobic. Everything started swirling into a tunnel, similar to the experience I'd had on the *Will Rogers* tour in Houston all those years ago. Ted was saying something, but I couldn't hear him. The food arrived, but I couldn't eat. I was too upset. At my body for failing me. That it took me so long to find Ted and that when I finally did and we wanted to start a family, we couldn't. That *I* couldn't. I thought something was wrong with me. Maybe my mother was right. I was still angry that it wasn't as easy as I had thought it would be. The maelstrom of emotions made me want to hurl myself out the window into the neon, blinking cityscape. I wanted to just disappear.

"Are you okay?" Ted asked.

Instead of answering, I left the table and made my way back to our room. I could feel all these feelings whirling within me and funneling up toward my chest. As soon as I opened the door, I began to wail. Was my body not cooperating for a reason? Was I that scared to become a mother because I thought I would become *my* mother? All the hope, all those dreams, all my insistence that I could do this came crashing down as I collapsed on the bed in a flood of tears.

Ted arrived moments later and found me sobbing into a pillow. I didn't even look up at him. I just wailed, curled up in the fetal position, "I hate this! Why is it all on me? All you have to do is jerk off in a cup. It all falls on the woman!"

I was ranting and sobbing, and I felt the pressure of *Younger* as well as *Sweet Charity* looming on the horizon.

"I can't do this alone. It can't just be on me!"

The tears were a truth serum. That lingering feeling that I had kept at bay was now on full display: I was not getting pregnant. This was not working.

"We have to explore other options," I said, still crying. "We have to pursue adoption."

Ted was rubbing my back, his big strong

hands soothing me. "Okay," he said. No sigh. No pushback. "Let's do it."

We had talked about it as a possibility, but he had been hesitant. His mom had an adopted sister, and that was a complicated relationship. And he had another friend who had a difficult time with his adoption. I understood why he was tentative. Meanwhile, my two best friends—Stephanie and Julien—were adopted. They were two of the four people in my totem pole–inspired drawing. The one drawing I did not include in the show. The one I planned to keep for my miracle baby.

"I'll do one more round of IVF, but you have to call Peter Hermann!" I said. "Talk to him!"

Peter and I had spoken briefly about adoption as a possibility. He offered to talk to us about their experience if we needed it. At that moment, we did. My body was telling me something profound. It was not cooperating. I had to think of different ways to remove the obstacles that were preventing me from becoming a mother.

That same night, Ted called Peter, and

they had a long conversation. Peter gave Ted the name and number of an adoption lawyer.

The next morning, I awoke and the sun was shining. It was a new day. I was exhausted from the crying and the waiting and the failing. But I had a small flicker of hope once again.

Maybe this would work.

Maybe the gods had another plan for me.

Maybe this journey was not so much about removing obstacles as it was about exploring new possibilities.

Maybe this was a new beginning.

BABY BLANKETS

Making My Own Patterns

I was in tech rehearsals for *Sweet Charity* when I got the call from the adoption lawyer to say she'd heard about a possibility.

We first met with her when we got back from Japan. During that intensive download, we learned that we needed to put together a brochure of the life we could offer a child. Our lawyer showed us examples of beautiful bound albums with color photos of hopeful parents, which are sent to birth mothers who ultimately choose whom they want to parent their child. This was news to me. I thought there was a giant database of babies and the lawyer just matched you up. What we learned is that in some cases, adoptive parents put ads in the paper to say they're looking for a child to adopt. That was how it was done prior to the internet: *PennySaver* and local papers. We also learned that we needed to fill out a ton of paperwork and meet with a social worker who would evaluate us, our home, and our living situation. And we had to take several online courses about adoption.

I left the lawyer's office feeling extremely overwhelmed and daunted.

Four weeks later, she called to say, "I heard about a situation. Get me all your material ASAP."

All the paperwork sat on our kitchen table untouched.

I called Ted in a panic. We had flipped through the forms and knew we had to write a letter to the potential birth mother to share our story about why we wanted to adopt, and why she should choose us to parent her child. It was so daunting to try to capture who we were and what type of life we could offer this unborn child. In a way, it was a blessing that we didn't have time to overthink it. And a blessing that I was married to a brilliant writer. Ted wrote that we had met later in life, so having a child of our own proved difficult, and that we felt like we could offer a loving, stable home for a baby, and a life full of joy and opportunity. He included all the pertinent details—that we were bicoastal, our ages, and that he was a writer and I was an actress, though he gave me a pseudonym. Then he printed out a few photos—one from our wedding, and another of us with our dog Mabel and our new dog Brody, a thirteen-pound Westie-poodle mix we'd adopted in the midst of our fertility struggles. We shoved all of that into a FedEx envelope and sent it to our lawyer.

Within a week, I learned that we were one of nine couples out of forty chosen to go to the next round. That was when I realized this was an audition. We got a call-back! Only this time, it was to be parents. I honestly couldn't believe it. After so many obstacles, doors were opening up. It truly felt like a new beginning.

Our lawyer forwarded us follow-up questions from the birth mother via email, and they struck both me and Ted as extremely thoughtful: Were we religious? How did we feel about vaccinations? Were we open to post-placement contact?

Ted and I looked at each other, amazed. These were important issues that we hadn't really thought of or talked about yet.

"What do you think she wants to hear?" I asked.

"We have to answer honestly," he said. "And hopefully our answers match up to hers."

So we did. We weren't religious. We were pro-vaccination. And we were very open to post-placement contact.

A day later, we found out it was down to three families.

Without giving away too many details, I will say that when Ted and I learned that the birth mother chose us, it felt very meant to be.

We picked the name Emily Dale: Emily for Ted's great-grandmother (he proposed to me with her ring), and Dale for my mother's middle name. She was due on March 15.

Adoption, they say, is not for the weary. Even though Emily's biological mom had already chosen us, we kept the news quiet. So many things can go wrong—this is true of pregnancy, and certainly of adoption. The birth mother can change her mind at any moment, all the way past her birth, which is her right. It varies state to state, as adoption is a legal transferal of parental guardianship, but it can take up to six months after the child is born. Ted and I understood that. It is a deeply intimate and personal relationship between the birth mother (or parents, if the father is involved) and the adoptive parents. They decide how and when to move forward, and I wanted to be very respectful of that. I also didn't want to get ahead of myself, so I didn't plan a nursery, or buy a stroller or a car seat. And unlike my determination when I was trying to get pregnant, I knew there was nothing I could do to control this process. I had to let go.

The anticipation was nerve-racking, so I funneled that energy into making a blanket—for Emily. I picked a very simple striped pattern from a baby blanket book, and then bought the softest yarn available, in cream and dusty rose. I worked in small bursts, often in my *Sweet Charity* dressing room, which I shared with Asmeret Ghebremichael, who played Nickie, and Emily Padgett, who played Helene.

Onstage, I was belting beloved Cy Coleman songs, like "If My Friends Could See Me Now" and "Where Am I Going?," and in between, I would crochet, like I had done so many times before. This time felt different.

One day, Asmeret asked, "What are you making?"

My body tensed—I had rehearsed this moment. "A baby blanket," I replied, in my calmest voice. I kept my eyes on the project in my lap: twelve rows done and forty more to go. Stitch by stitch, step by step, I was inching my way toward being a mother.

"Aw," she said. "So sweet. Who is it for?"

"Friends are expecting a baby girl," I said.

The only people who knew that I was the one expecting were my father, and my closest friends: Julien and Stephanie were my confidants and consultants from the start. I was so grateful to have them in my life offering their perspectives as I navigated my own road being an adoptive mom — and in Emily's life, so they could someday share their own adoption stories with her, as well. Megan knew, too. She'd come visit me at work, and I watched in amazement as her belly grew larger each time. Her due date was fast approaching: January 15, 2017. Our kids would be two months apart if things worked out. *If.*

We'd get giddy imagining how our lives were about to change over ramen or burgers at the Gotham West Market around the corner from the Signature Theatre, where *Sweet Charity* was playing. After all our planning and dreaming, there was a good chance we would have babies at the same time after all.

When I told my dad that he was going to be a grandpa, he smiled wide, showing all his new teeth. He knew that Ted and I had been trying for a while. He was scared that something might go wrong, that the birth mother would change her mind, or that it wouldn't all work out. He tried to protect me by telling me not to get my hopes up and to stay open and realistic. I could see how he was cautiously optimistic and also a little nervous. He even said that he kept having nightmares of dropping a baby down an elevator shaft.

It was around this same time that he introduced me to his new lady friend Marilyn. They had been dating a few months when they drove up from Florida to celebrate Thanksgiving with us. Prior to meeting her, he said, "She's nothing like your mother." They came to see me in the show, and I immediately understood what he meant. Marilyn struck me as a kind and generous person who was clearly crazy about my dad.

I continued to work on the baby blanket through December, and crocheting continued to ease the anxiety of what might happen—until one day, I just stopped. I was about three-fourths of the way done when a friend told me about how her adoption story hadn't worked out. The birth family changed their mind—after the hopeful parents had already come to the hospital and held the baby. In adoption, this is entirely possible. They were devastated— and I couldn't finish the blanket. I was too afraid. What if something went wrong? What would I do with the blanket? Maybe I was jinxing it.

Emily was still a figment of my imagination, and so making this very tangible thing to wrap around her felt like a fantasy. I placed the blanket, a soft version of a very faded candy cane, in a canvas tote and thought, *I'll finish it—one day.*

That January, we had an appointment for a social worker to visit our apartment in New York City. I was so nervous. What if she decided that we were unfit to be parents? But I was also glad that someone was checking us out and wished everyone was vetted that way. When Mabel and Brody swirled around the social worker's feet during the visit, I tensed up. What if dogs are a no-no? Would she judge us based on the way they behaved?

We were also taking online courses that explained the legal process of adoption, as well as the emotional process for the birth parents, the adoptive parents, and ultimately the child. In one of the videos, the narrator said that there were often magical signs between the birth mom and the adoptive parents that help you know when it is meant to be. By then, the lawyer had put me in direct contact with Emily's birth mom, and we began to email back and forth. At first, it was very straightforward, just getting to know each other. *How was your day? How are you feeling?* But then there were a few things that she mentioned that made me feel like this was meant to be. We had shared family birthdays and even middle names. She loved musical theater.

A few emails later, she wrote that she was making a blanket for the baby.

A chill ran through my body as I typed back, "Oh, do you knit?"

"No," she responded. "It's crochet."

My heart was skipping and fluttery at once as I typed back to her, "I crochet, too!"

"I'm not very good," she replied. "I'm making a ton of mistakes. But it's a great way for me to focus my energy."

I was laughing as I wrote her back to say, "That's all part of it! I'm crocheting a blanket for her, too!"

A sign.

When *Sweet Charity* closed, Ted and I decided to take a vacation to Key West for our last hurrah as a childless couple—or so we hoped. On our fourth day, I awoke to a text from Megan: "My water broke at 2am and I'm at the hospital! He's on his way."

I immediately booked a flight back to NYC and headed straight from the airport to the hospital to meet Beckett Gwynn Halpin, born January 15, 2017. When I arrived in Megan's room, she was in bed staring at this tiny baby lying in the hospital bassinet. She looked tired but happy.

"How do you feel?" I asked her.

"Like an alien is in the room," she said. "I know I carried him for nine months but it's just so surreal to have him suddenly here."

I held little Beckett and understood what she meant: he was so tiny and cute, and making all these squeaky new-baby noises. I was mesmerized—until he began to cry!

I handed him back to Megan, panicked. Was he hungry? Tired? Gassy? Neither of us knew, and we laughed about the inevitable learning curve of new motherhood. I could not yet believe I was about to embark on it.

Emily was due in two months, and I tried my best to keep busy. I had a concert planned in Rochester that February. Beckett was three weeks old, but Megan insisted on coming. She often joined me onstage to sing "Flight," and she was so determined to get back to work that three weeks after giving birth via C-section, Adam drove her and Beckett six hours in our VW Tiguan (packed to the gills with a ton of baby stuff!) so she could perform. She wanted to prove to herself that she could have a child and continue with her career. Four weeks later, family in tow, she did it again, this time driving ten hours to Ohio to sing with me and the Cincinnati Pops. This was hugely important for me to witness, as I planned to continue performing as well. I saw Megan doing it and kept thinking, *Wow, working moms are total badasses!*

I was back in New York on March 4, working with Michael Rafter on some new music for a concert planned at Lincoln Center in April. The birth mom had already had a couple of false alarms, so I knew the baby's arrival was imminent. I was a messy mix of emotions: excited about the possibility of becoming a mother, scared that my life was about to change forever, and triple-terrified that it all might fall apart. Megan asked if I wanted a baby shower, and I said no. I didn't want to jinx anything. I was desperately just trying to stay calm. I was too wound up to even crochet. Instead, I focused on searching for new music for the show.

Michael had an idea of doing a mashup of two songs: "Take Me to the World" by Stephen Sondheim, and "Starting Here, Starting Now" by Richard Maltby Jr. and David Shire. The first piece was a wistful ballad of longing that built into the second song, a triumphant declaration of what will be. Michael began to play the music for this yearning song, and a wave of emotion swept over me. I could feel little doors in my heart being flung open to make room for *her* as I sang, "Take me to the world that's real. Show me how it's done. Teach me how to laugh, to feel."

I had sung this before and never really understood it. Suddenly, it was so clear.

"This song is about her," I said to Michael.

"I know," he said, smiling.

I can't explain it, other than to say all the anticipation I had been feeling peaked—and released—as I sang this song. That was when I knew: Emily was on her way.

On my way home from the rehearsal studio, I called Megan in a panic.

"Megan! I don't want to get ahead of myself, but we have literally not gotten one thing yet—what are the ten things I need for a newborn? What can't you live without for Beckett?"

"I'll email you," she said. I could hear Beckett screaming in the background. Before we hung up, she added, "You got this!"

That evening, I opened the email with Megan's list:

1. stroller
2. car seat

3. bassinet/Rock 'n Play (which has since been deemed dangerous, FYI!)
4. changing pad
5. newborn diapers
6. onesies
7. wipes
8. swaddle blankets
9. formula
10. bottles

I had knots in my stomach as I printed the list. All I had was an unfinished baby blanket and a wide-open heart.

Ted and I went to Buy Buy Baby that afternoon, and I raced through the aisles grabbing all the things on the list. Ted thought I was a little crazy to insist that it all had to be done *that moment*, but it helped calm me down knowing that we at least had a way to transport her once she arrived. Also, diapers. We then stuffed all these totally foreign objects in the back of our Tiguan.

That night, Megan and Adam brought Beckett over to watch a movie with our friends Tony and Rob, both of whom are incredibly handy. Ted and I were walking in circles around all the boxes and bags of baby gear, both too on edge and nervous to sit down, let alone start piecing together baby equipment. As soon as they walked in the door, I said, "For the sake of our marriage, will you please put the stroller together for us?"

Thankfully, they were thrilled to be part of what we hoped would be a welcome-home celebration. There were another ten days before Emily's due date, but I had a feeling she would come early. Megan and Adam put Beckett down in Ted's office (Emily's soon-to-be nursery) and then we watched *Two for the Road*, in which Audrey Hepburn and Albert Finney play a couple examining their twelve-year relationship while on a road trip in France. That movie is about stages of marriage: courtship, honeymoon, malaise, dysfunction, parenthood, reconciliation. Ted and I joked that we were on the razor's edge of transitioning from one stage to another: *Three for the Road!*

Halfway through the movie, I had another panic.

"What if the baby comes in the middle of the night?" I said to Ted, in front of all our friends.

I could tell by the way he looked at me that he thought I was being insane—but then Megan nodded (bless her!), and Ted went down to make sure our car was easily available. We were planning to drive to the hospital, which was at least five hours away. Our garage closed at 10:00 p.m. and wouldn't open again until 7:00 a.m.

We got the call the following morning—at 6:58 a.m.

Emily was on her way.

We grabbed Mabel and Brody and all the shit we had bought at Buy Buy Baby and climbed into the car. The next thing I knew, I was at the hospital holding six-pound, thirteen-ounce Emily, this perfect little bundle of adorableness. It was the first baby I'd held that I couldn't pass off to their mother, because the mother was me! No one can prepare you for that moment: terrifying and thrilling. Every single moment from then on is brand new and unknown.

Since she was born in a different state, we

had to stay there until all the legal paper-work had been filed. We booked a room at a Residence Inn, similar to the one my family had lived in when I was thirteen and had just moved to Detroit. Of course, this was so very different.

When they let us take Emily from the hospital I was like, *You're just gonna let us leave? With a baby?* Ted buckled her car seat into the back of our car, and I proudly put a *Baby on Board* sticker on the back windshield. I sat next to her, staring at her darling little face, feeling every bump and turn in new ways. When Ted asked, "Wanna go through the Starbucks drive-through?," I was jolted. "Are we allowed to do that?" I replied.

Since we were stuck for a while in our Residence Inn, my dad and Marilyn drove up from Florida, and Megan, Adam, and Beckett took the train from NYC to spend a few of those early sweet days with us. Three months earlier, we were eating ramen and pontificating about what motherhood would be like. Now, we were sitting together in the hotel room, holding our babies. We still tell people that Beckett is Emily's oldest friend. He was two months old, and Emily just three days old, on their first play date.

"You did it," Megan said. "You got your family. And look at us! We're doing it together."

I still couldn't believe it. I suddenly realized that the gods hadn't let me down. They were patiently waiting for me to get out of their way so that they could lead me to Emily. I had to let go of whatever I had planned in my head. The reason none of it was working was because it already *was* working. Emily was on her way to us. Emily was my story.

We stayed in that Residence Inn for ten days, waiting for all the paperwork to be complete before we could start our drive back to NYC: my precious little family.

The drive home took much longer, as Ted drove at about 35 miles per hour. I savored every minute. One fun fact? Emily's umbilical cord stub popped off while I was changing her diaper in an I-95 rest-stop bathroom. Again, nothing prepares you for motherhood!

When we got back to the apartment, the doormen were shocked to see us walk in with a baby. Emily had been this big secret! I hadn't even told my *Younger* castmates. I just sent them a photo of me holding Emily with the caption "Guess what!?"

Three weeks after she was born, I had to go back to work shooting season four of *Younger*. Megan had gone back to work when Beckett was that young; I could do it as well! Instead of finishing the baby blanket I had started, I was inspired to make something new now that she was finally here. I was grateful for my work, but I knew I would be away from her for hours at a time—I wanted something that I could pour my love into. I picked out a pattern for a very charming crocheted blanket that I found online. It had nine squares, each in a pastel color, with a number in the center.

In the past, crochet was an outlet for me to pour my pain and heartbreak and anxiety and despair into. It helped stitch me together in times of great turmoil and pain. Now I was pouring love and comfort (and just a touch of nervous new-mom energy) into this new blanket, the first I made since my daughter had arrived.

The first panel was pink. The numeral 1 was made with a popcorn stitch, which creates what look like raised, soft marbles of yarn. Each number was made this way, so that they rose off the blanket base, giving the blanket a nubby texture. The number 2 was a lime green, the 3 a lemony yellow, the 4 a sky blue, and the 5 a lavender purple. The remaining numbers 6 through 9 mirrored 1 through 4. And since I wanted it to be perfect, I must have redone each panel two or three times until I got it just right. Everyone on the set was super invested in my progress. People would pop their heads into my dressing room to ask, "What number are you working on today?"

Both Ted and I worked full-time, so we hired a night nurse who basically saved our asses. Neither of us knew how to take care of a baby—I had changed a diaper (thanks to Stephanie!) but had never burped a baby, and neither had Ted. I was learning fundamental things in real time: how to swaddle Emily, feed her, dress her, bathe her. This was a different kind of learning curve, and I remember holding her one day and thinking, *What took me so long?*

Ted so clearly felt the same, and my love for him deepened through his love for her. He'd sing, in all of his tone-deaf glory, "Emily" by Johnny Mercer and Johnny Mandel, which Tony Bennett made famous: "Emily, Emily, Emily has the murmuring sound of May." He'd kiss her all over her dark-brown hair in between each verse through to the end: "As my eyes visualize a family, they see Emily, Emily."

We were surrounded by magic and music and sweet Emily smiles.

Inspired by Megan, I started bringing Emily to work. Iyeika, our baby nurse, would hang with her in my dressing room, where Miriam Shor and Hilary Duff would come and play with (or just hold) her. The love triangle between the characters Liza, Charles, and Josh was in full swing onscreen that season, but between hot and heavy takes, Peter Hermann and Nico Tortorella would be doing tummy time with Emily on her *Finding Nemo* play mat. Darren Star bought Em a travel crib so she could nap in my dressing room, and Debi Mazar bought her tiny gold Gucci shoes.

Even with help, I was sleep-deprived and distracted. I was working fourteen-hour days on set and wanted every moment with Emily to count. As soon as I was home from work, I shifted into mom mode, taking her for walks in her giant, dark-green Uppababy stroller, dragging poor Mabel and Brody behind me. I'd come home and lay her in her DockATot on the kitchen table and play the Beatles while I folded laundry. Emily was a pretty remarkable baby: she wasn't too fussy. When she did cry, the only thing that would calm her down was if I blasted opera. It would literally stun her into silence. She was inherently independent, preferring not to be held but to be snuggled in her swaddle so she could watch the world on her own terms.

I used to be on time or early for every appointment, and now I was consistently fifteen minutes late for everything—mainly because I was always scrambling to make sure I had everything I needed in my giant

diaper backpack that I carried everywhere—
in addition to my usual nut bar and bottle
of water, there were diapers, wipes, a bottle,
a pacifier, and a change of tiny clothes in
case of a blowout! I was also used to knowing all my lines and being super prepared
for work, but now my brain was foggy. My
priorities had shifted. I thought my work
would suffer, but oddly, it was better. My
home life was so full that it infused my
work life with new layers of meaning. We
were creating new patterns every single
minute.

Emily was four months old when she
took her first plane trip. I had a concert in
Boone, North Carolina, not far from where
my Aunt Mary Anne lives. Em and Ted
came with me, and we all had the loveliest
family reunion. My dad's sister Linda came
with my Great-Uncle Ken, as did Mary
Anne and her husband, my Uncle Mike,
along with their kids, my cousins.

It was on that trip that Mary Anne gave me
a corner-to-corner ("C2C" in crochet-ese)
crocheted blanket in rainbow stripes. It was
the first time I had ever seen that design—

the stripes were catty-corner instead of straight up and down, which is next-level crochet. Aunt Mary Anne also told me she had joined a crochet club called Chicks with Sticks through her church, and all I could think was *I want to be her when I grow up!* #Goals.

I returned to New York inspired. After I finished the numbers blanket, I found my next pattern on *Repeat Crafter Me,* a crochet blog I follow whose author has a daughter a few years older than Emily. She posts tons of cute patterns and ideas for kids—and that was where I saw a C2C owl baby blanket. When Emily was born, Ted and I called her our little owl. That wise, chubby bird has shown up throughout my life: in the squares I crocheted for my mom in the last days of her life, in the drawing of myself and my chosen family as animals, and now, with this wide-eyed (and nocturnal!) wonder who had landed in our life. Ted and I always joke that when Emily was born, she looked up at both of us with her gigantic eyes as if to say, "I got this. You both are idiots."

I had never done corner-to-corner crochet before, and it made me feel connected to Aunt Mary Anne. Usually, in crochet, you work from side to side, but with C2C you work diagonally. The pattern follows a colored graph and looks very similar to cross-stitch, except in C2C each square represents a collection of four stitches. You begin in the corner with four stitches, making one "square." The next diagonal is two squares, then three, then four, etc. I used Vanna's Choice yarn from Lion Brand. (Fun fact: The *Wheel of Fortune* hostess has her own collection of yarn with Lion Brand. How cool is that? That has become my go-to yarn, because who doesn't love Vanna White?)

Following this pattern led me to my next crochet epiphany: maybe I could create my own graph! Up until that point, I had always followed someone else's pattern. Other than choosing the colors, I never veered from it. The zigzag blanket, the butterfly blanket, the divorce blanket, the owl blanket. For every single one, I followed a specific pattern, usually one I found in *Crochet Today!* I had no idea that I could crochet what is called a "graphghan" (graph + afghan) using my own patterns created with whatever images I wanted.

That led me to the next milestone moment in my crochet career: What if I took one of my drawings and turned it into a pattern for a blanket? Mind explosion. This opened up a whole new creative process.

My first graphghan was a penguin. I drew the plump black-and-white bird out on regular paper, then transferred it to graph paper and colored it in: black wings, white belly, and tiny orange beak. I had no idea if it would work, but as I began to crochet the blanket, the image started to emerge. There it was, little by little, stitch by stitch. What I had drawn was now a crocheted little blanket. The possibilities were endless.

With Emily in our lives, we were literally creating new patterns every day—why couldn't that translate into my crochet? I didn't have to follow anyone else's instructions. I could make my own. I was so inspired that my New Year's resolution for 2018 was to create ten original baby blankets. And I did:

1. A giraffe.
2. A sea turtle, based on a drawing I had done.
3. A bunny—the background is a variegated yarn in pastel pinks, yellows, and purples.
4. Ganesh, based on the fertility drawing I had done before Emily arrived.
5. A badass baby blanket, with the word *BADASS* in all capitals, just like the collage—because you're never too young to be one! (I now want an adult-sized version.)
6. A hot-pink dinosaur. I distinctly remember making out with Peter Hermann on set and crocheting this in between scenes.
7. An octopus, inspired by one of Emily's ABC baby books (O was for octopus).
8. A llama, which I gave to Hilary Duff, who was pregnant in season five. She loves llamas and even has a real one! His name is Ivan.
9. A lion. Because, like Vanna

White, I developed a relationship with Lion Brand Yarn. I posted a picture of me working on the *BADASS* baby blanket on Instagram, and someone from the company wrote in my comments: "We want to send you some yarn." I was so excited! A few days later, a magical box filled with twenty-five balls of yarn arrived in my dressing room, and I practically hyperventilated.

10. Three little birds, as in the Bob Marley song, because "every little thing is going to be all right." And it *was*.

In fact, it was more than all right; it was freeing and fantastic. Motherhood was exhausting and wonderful and completely new. But the love I feel for Emily overwhelmed any of the anxieties I had about being a mother. I was so worried that my complicated relationship with my own mother, the conflicts and struggles and her underlying mental illness, would somehow taint my own ability to become a parent. But with Emily, I saw how I could be my own kind of mother. I was free. I didn't have to keep repeating the same pattern. I could create my own.

On Emily's first birthday, her birth mother came to celebrate with us. She gave Emily the crocheted blanket she'd made while she was pregnant. It was hot pink and bright blue. All these vibrant gorgeous colors. It was so beautiful, mainly because it was made with such love. And then I noticed that hers, like mine, wasn't finished either. I asked her why not, and she said, "I don't know how to weave in the ends."

I told her I hadn't finished my blanket for Emily either—and promised her that I would weave in the ends for both of us. But mostly for Emily.

BADASS BABY BLANKET

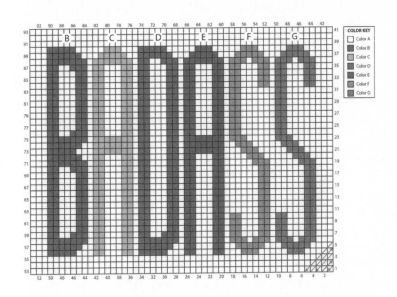

SKILL LEVEL

Intermediate

SIZE

About 29 x 38 in. (73.5 x 96.5 cm)
41 x 53 squares

MATERIALS

- **Lion Brand® Vanna's Choice® (Art. #860)**
- #099 Linen 6 balls (A)
- #180 Cranberry 1 ball (B)
- #172 Kelly Green 1 ball (C)
- #174 Olive 1 ball (D)
- #116 Orion Blue 2 balls (E)
- #135 Rust 1 ball (F)
- #113 Scarlet 1 ball (G)
- **Lion Brand® crochet hook size H-8 (5 mm)**
- **Lion Brand® large-eyed blunt needle**

GAUGE

- 6 (chain 3, 3 dc) squares = about 4 in. (10 cm).
- 1 square = about 0.67 in. (1.7 cm).
- BE SURE TO CHECK YOUR GAUGE.

TECHNIQUE EXPLANATIONS

C2C The corner-to-corner (C2C) technique of crocheting is made by starting in one corner of a pixel graph (the lower right corner) and following the graph row by row diagonally to the other corner (the top left corner).

How to Start Your C2C Blanket

Row 1: Begin in the bottom right corner of the graph. Chain 6. DC in 4th chain from hook. DC in last 2 chains. You now have a chain-3 space and a total of 3 DC stitches. This completes your first square and Row 1.

Row 2: Chain 6. DC in 4th chain from hook. DC in last 2 chains. Turn your work. At this point turning consists of just flipping over the first square. Slip stitch to join to the chain-3 space from the first square. Chain 3. Make 3 DC in the same chain-3 space. This completes your second 2 squares and Row 2.

Continue by chaining 6, DC in 3rd chain from hook and in last 2 chains, turn and join with slip stitch to chain-3 space in last square made from previous row.

Increase Rows The first part of the graph is worked by making increases on both edges. You will start each row by chaining 6, making a DC in the 4th chain from hook and then a DC in each of the remaining 2 chains.

Increase and Decrease Rows　The second part of the graph is worked by making increases on one edge and making decreases on the other edge.

How to Decrease at the Beginning of a Row　Slip stitch in the 3 double crochet stitches from last square made. Slip stitch to join to the chain-3 from last square made. Chain 3. Make 3 DC in chain-3 space. Continue making squares as you have been doing (slip stitch to join to chain-3 space then chain 3 and work 3 DC in the same chain-3 space).

How to Decrease at the End of a Row　Make squares as you have been doing up to the last chain-3 space. Slip stitch in the last chain-3 space but do not work chain 3 and 3 DC in that last chain-3 space. Turn and proceed with the next row.

Decrease Rows　The third part of the graph is worked by making decreases on both edges. At the beginning of each row, instead of chaining 6 as you would do when increasing, you will turn your work and slip stitch across the 3 DC's in the last square made. Join with slip st to the chain-3 then chain 3 and work 3 DC in the same chain-3 space. At the end of the row, end with a slip stitch in the last chain-3 space; do not work chain 3 and 3 DC in that last chain-3 space.

How to Change Colors To join a new color, pull the new color yarn through as you make your slip stitch to join over your chain-3 space. Do not fasten off the old color. Leave the strand hanging and still attached to the ball.

By not cutting the yarn each time you change colors, you'll have fewer loose ends to weave in later. Just keep the balls not being used on the wrong side of your work. Carry the yarn strand up from the previous row and pull it up to your hook when you need to join that color back into your project.

When you begin to have a lot of color changes, it helps to divide the yarn balls by winding into multiple smaller balls.

How to Read the Graph

Print out the graph. Start in the lower right corner and mark off each square as you go. Each square in this C2C graph = chain 3 + 3 DC. The first square in the corner is Row 1. You will work diagonally back and forth (down one row and back up the next). Row 2 of the graph will be read diagonally from left to right and Row 3 from right to left.

BLANKET

Work in C2C technique, changing yarn color following chart.
Fasten off.

FINISHING

Edging

From RS, join E with sl st anywhere along outside edge of Afghan.

Rnd 1: Ch 1, working around outer edge of afghan, work 1 sc in each DC and base ch, 3 sc in each ch-3 sp, and 3 sc in each corner; join with sl st in first sc.

Rnds 2 and 3: Ch 1, sc in each st around working 3 sc in center st at each corner; join with sl st in first sc.

Fasten off.

Weave in ends.

ABBREVIATIONS

ch = chain
ch-sp(s) = chain spaces previously made
DC = double crochet
rnd(s) = round(s)
RS = right side
sc = single crochet
sl st = slip stitch
st(s) = stitch(es)

Every effort has been made to produce accurate and complete instructions. We cannot be responsible for variance of individual crafters, human error, or typographical mistakes.

HOOKED

Crafting a Book about Crafting

Shortly after my mom died, my agent Joe sent me the pilot script of a new television show called *Younger*, about a forty-year-old mom who poses as a twentysomething in order to get a job in the publishing industry, written by Darren Star. I'd never really watched *Sex and the City*, which Darren had also created. It came out at a time in my life when I didn't relate to it. I didn't know anyone like the four women in that show. I was so naïve and young, and a lot of the subject matter was too racy. Samantha's jokes flew over my head, and I couldn't relate to Carrie's fashion sense at all. Still, I knew who Darren Star was and was excited to read the script.

Bunheads had been canceled, and I was engaged and living in LA with Ted. *Violet* was a possibility, but not yet confirmed, so I didn't know what was next for me. Truthfully, I was a little lost.

I started reading the *Younger* script standing up at my kitchen counter—and I didn't sit down till I finished the script. I immediately called Joe.

"I have to do this pilot," I said.

It was smart and funny and spoke to me directly, as I felt like I was at a place in my career where I was falling between the cracks age-wise. I still "looked young" at thirty-eight, but I had never had a role where this worked to my advantage in such a specific way. Also, just like in *Bunheads*, there was a theme of reinvention that appealed to me. I felt like I knew who this woman was.

And often, when I read scripts or look at new projects, I get excited about who's involved. Getting to work with Darren Star felt thrilling. We met for lunch at a restaurant somewhere in Hollywood, and I showed up as me: no makeup, in a white

T-shirt and jeans. It was pleasant—I learned that he was a big Broadway fan and had seen *Anything Goes*—but by the end of the lunch, I wasn't sure if I'd made a good enough impression on him.

A few days later, Joe called to tell me that TV Land, the network producing *Younger*, wanted me to do a screen test. I really wanted this job. I had to prepare scenes for the audition. One was the opening scene of the pilot, in which forty-year-old Liza walks into a publishing house and tries to get a job. Another was Liza pretending to be her younger self. I pulled out a black Dolce and Gabbana dress I had worn for publicity during *Anything Goes* for my "younger" look and bought a simple tweed jacket from a thrift store on Ventura for my "older" look. I hired someone to do my hair and makeup. I wasn't going to risk it.

The audition was at CBS Studio Center, which is about five minutes from my house in Los Angeles. Darren was there with a few other folks. I was really excited, because I thought this was a job I actually might be right for. And I was right!

A week later, Joe called: I got the part.

My first thought was *I wish I could tell my mom.* It was the first job I got that she didn't know about. She had found so many opportunities for me when I was young— and kept such close tabs on me throughout my career—that I couldn't help but think she had something to do with this one, too. I attributed it to her pulling some strings up in heaven. I felt like being cast as Liza was a gift from her.

Thanks, Mom.

Bunheads was baptism by fire—I learned hard and fast the basics of how to be on a TV show. On *Younger*, I was able to figure out how to act in front of a camera, and how to be an integral part of the cast and crew that creates the magic that was this particular show for seven seasons, which also paralleled the best years of my life. The two are connected.

The very first time I stepped into a real publishing house was when I pitched this book idea, six seasons into the show. On *Younger*, my character was originally hired as a marketing assistant at the fictional

publishing house Empirical, but gets pro-
moted to editor as the seasons progress. Fun
fact: I had never actually met a *real* editor,
so I didn't know what to expect when I
walked into that first meeting. I had never
pitched a book before; I had just watched
actors on our show pitch—and publish—
crazy book ideas with hilarious titles. Think
Little Women in Space, *Dead Cat Bounce*,
and *P Is for Pigeon*. A book about crafting
that really tells the story of my agoraphobic
mother didn't seem too far-fetched!

On our set, we called the room where such
meetings took place the "conference room
of death," because it was so hot, plus it took
forever to shoot a scene there; the room was
surrounded by glass and so, like with *Bunheads*, the camera operators were always
trying to avoid filming their reflections. As
a result, every conference room scene took
five to six hours to shoot, and we'd all be
delirious and either get the giggles or flub
our lines. (They eventually got smart and
added frosted glass squares to break up the
reflection. You can see the difference in
season two.) To be in a conference room

without cameras, pitching a book about how crochet saved my life, was a bizarre thrill. As it turned out, the publishing world loved *Younger*, and the idea for this book! We had thirteen pitch meetings all over Manhattan.

When I walked into Grand Central Publishing, the last place we pitched, I thought, *Oh my God, it looks just like the Empirical set.* Beautiful books lining the walls on wooden bookshelves, framed book jackets hanging proudly on the walls. I walked into the gorgeous, air-conditioned conference room and explained my thoughts for this book to Ben Sevier, the publisher, and several other people from the office, including Suzanne O'Neill, the woman who became my editor.

I knew I needed help pretty much right away. I'm surrounded by talented writers. My husband, Ted Griffin, is a screenwriter, best known for writing the *Ocean's Eleven* script. Hunter, true to my mother's prediction, is a brilliant writer. And I was on a show written by one of the most successful writers in the TV industry. I know how hard they work at their craft, and I didn't treat the opportunity casually. I approached it in the way I am most familiar and comfortable with—coming from the world of theater and having worked with Michael Rafter on evenings of song, I wanted a collaborator. Someone who could help me get the story that was in my head onto the page.

Enter the amazing Liz Welch.

When we first met, it felt very meant to be. We had a lot in common. We had both adopted our daughters and were on our second marriages, and bonus: Liz had worked with Peter Hermann at *Vanity Fair*! This was also her eighth book—her first was a memoir called *The Kids Are All Right*, which was about losing her mother at a young age. (Her mother also happened to be an actress who left college after her first year to go on tour with *The Pajama Game*.) She does not crochet (yet!), but she does love dogs.

We started this process back in 2018, when I was doing a two-week run at the Café Carlyle. She came to meet me at the hotel, and we began by talking about my life as a performer chronologically—starting with when and where I was born—and then adding each craft as I learned it. It took a while to wrestle that story onto the page, which read more like a memoir with a peppering of crafts throughout it. That was not what I had pitched, nor was it the story I wanted to tell. We did a 180 and broke down pieces of my life through the lens of the particular objects that I had made. The first part that we wrote was "Badass," as that collage, and Patti LuPone's influence, were such a perfect example of what I wanted this book to be about.

Figuring out how to tell this story coincided with the last season of *Younger*—and the coronavirus pandemic. Shooting began in October 2020 and continued through February 2021. And I worked on this book every day while we were filming. Liz would send me her edits and notes on the chapters, writing her questions IN ALL CAPS, which I would answer directly in the manuscript, adding my thoughts, feelings, and memories in between shooting scenes. That meant darting off into an empty room, sometimes that damn conference room. Everyone at work had watched me crochet for the first six seasons—now, they would find me on the sets for Maggie's loft or Liza's office, typing away on my little pink MacBook Air.

"What are you working on now?" was a question I often got.

"A book! About crafting!" I would say.

Writing, like crochet, singing, drawing, and acting, is also a craft. And just like with each of those creative processes, some days you wake up inspired and everything gels! Other days, you just stare at the screen for hours. Sometimes, you have to start over completely, and every once in a while, your work doesn't save (*the worst*).

But Liz helped me find and follow my story and encouraged me to dig deeper. We always knew we were on to something if she got goose bumps (or cried). My editor, Suzanne, put the magnifying glass on our words, was a stickler for repetition, and always wanted a scene. She challenged me to really home in on exactly what I wanted to say—and why.

This was hard work, and *Younger* was the perfect backdrop. Beyond the irony of working on my own book while playing an editor at a fake publishing house, there was so much drama to untangle in my own life story—and there was no way I could have done it without such a loving and support- ive work environment. It was the opposite of "Basket Case," where cross-stitch saved me from tricky cast dynamics. This time, *writing* was the challenge, while the cast was great! We truly loved and respected one another.

We shot seven seasons over seven years, and we all had major life moments along the way: Hilary got divorced, got pregnant, got remarried, and got pregnant again. Nico got married. Molly fell in love and is engaged. I got married and became a mother—something I had in common with Miriam and Debi, who both have two daughters. Peter Hermann has three kids and, as you now know, played a key role in our adoption story.

Every year, for seven years, we would all come together to shoot this show. We'd work crazy hours, do crazy things (like shooting an entire scene in a bubble bath with Nico), and act in so many crazy storylines! If my mom were alive to see Thad get killed by a falling construction beam, her email would have said, "I told you so!" I have no idea how she would have reacted to Lauren's vagina getting stuck to that ice sculpture...but I digress. The point is, when we wrapped, we always had the next season to look forward to. Now that it has ended, I am both sad and grateful.

The cast had that elusive thing called chemistry. Debi intimidated me at first—until I learned that she's a softy with a tough exterior. Some of my favorite days were just the two of us on the loft set, made even better if I got to be in sweatpants, my hair pulled into a messy bun on top of my head. That was my idea of comfy. Hers was a flowing Gucci robe, a turban, big gold hoops, and heeled mules. If you've ever wondered if people really wear that when they're just lounging around in their apartment, the answer is yes—if you're Debi.

It took a little longer for me and Hilary

to bond. We always got along, but it wasn't until I became a mom that we became really close. We would talk about all of our trials and triumphs. I would ask her advice, and we'd lament sleepless nights. I also respected how she handled her career so beautifully. She navigated her celebrity with such grace and humility. I never once saw her turn down a fan if they approached while we were filming (which was often). She was always willing to take a picture or autograph something. She even dealt with the paparazzi, who were relentless with her.

When we shot the pilot, I noticed an anchor tattoo on her ankle.

"So I'll always stay grounded," she explained.

Throughout the seasons, she dabbled with knitting, but during season seven, I converted her to crochet. This is one of my prouder achievements.

Molly, who played the hilarious pill-popping millennial fashion publicist Lauren, started crocheting, too. For my wrap gift, she gave me a little bag to hold all my crochet hooks. It had *CCPrez* (Crochet Club President) embroidered on it in gold lettering.

Molly, Hilary, and I would sit together between scenes and crochet, with me giving them ideas and tips. Molly was really intimidated at first, so I told her to take it slow and try not to get frustrated or impatient. Equally important, she had to figure out how to hold the hook, as everyone holds it in their own way—there is no "right" way. She got the hang of it quickly and started making hats and scarves nonstop! A natural!

Molly asked me early on how I navigate the workplace and learning lines and the pressures of being on a TV show. I told her that crochet has helped me throughout my entire career by giving my brain and my hands something to do other than worrying about what people might be saying. And that was way better for me than mindlessly looking at my phone and the noise of social media (message boards on *steroids*).

Molly really took to crochet and now has this tool in her arsenal as she heads off to do other things. Fun fact: Molly told me that she wrote me a fan letter when she was a teenager after she saw *Thoroughly Modern Millie* and that I sent her a headshot that said, "Follow your dreams." I love that I may have been her Patti.

Peter Hermann is also a wonderful human being—and the best gift giver ever! When we wrapped season one, he gave me two copies of *Anna Karenina*, as I had mentioned that Ted and I were thinking about starting a husband-and-wife book club and both wanted to read it. Peter remembered—and while we haven't read them yet (sorry, Peter!), we will. After season two, he had a baseball cap made for me that said MAYOR. I had shared with him Ted's advice to me before we started production: Liza was the lead in the series (number one on the call sheet), which he equated with being the "mayor," meaning it was my job to set an optimistic, happy tone on set. That reminded me of *Millie*. I took that responsibility very seriously—we work long hours, and so I made it a point to always be kind, and prepared.

Peter and I were the last cast members standing when we wrapped season seven at 4:30 a.m. on February 25, 2021. It was freezing, and we were on the sidewalk outside of the Bowery Ballroom. Our first AD, Jennifer Truelove, was wearing the crocheted rainbow leg warmers I'd made for her when she announced: "And that's a *series* wrap on *Younger*."

It felt so finite. I had already said good-bye to Nico, Hilary, Debi, and Molly, and had cried all my tears. At that moment, I just felt enormous gratitude. I said a few words, along the lines of "I feel like the luckiest person. Thank you for an amazing seven years."

Peter gave a beautiful speech, in which he called me a weaver—not just of yarn, but of people. I was so moved. I equated that to being a good mayor. He then handed me a folded-up piece of fabric and said, "My last words are 'thank you.' And I wanted to say it in your language." I unfurled this beautiful burlap banner to reveal giant crocheted letters that spelled out the words THANK YOU in purple, gold, orange, and cream. I held it up for everyone to see, beaming. It was the most thoughtful gift ever.

As we were saying our final goodbyes, I asked Peter where he found such a beautiful piece of crochet.

He flashed his megawatt smile and said, "I made it!"

I was stunned. "*What?*" I may have even shouted.

"I've been watching you crochet for seven seasons, so I went to Knitty City on the Upper West Side and took lessons from this little old lady, and I watched a few YouTube videos, too. Didn't you wonder why I wasn't sitting in the same room as you the other day when we were shooting? I was furiously trying to finish the rest of your present."

That was one of the many gifts I got while being on *Younger*. I look back on those seven years and remember so many highlights.

Nico and I got really close. On *Younger*, Nico plays a male character, but in real life they're nonbinary and use the pronouns "they" and "them." One of my favorite memories was when we were shooting in

Ireland during season four. Nico and I decided to go on a cross-country road trip to Galway. People drive on the opposite side of the street there, so I asked, "Nico, have you ever driven on the left side of the road before?"

They flashed their own megawatt smile and said, "No, but I can figure it out!"

I could hear my mother's voice saying, "Don't you dare get into that car!"

But I trusted Nico, and they did a pretty good job, even though I kept screaming, "Left, left," convinced we were going to crash. On that trip, we had a long talk about sexuality—what it meant to be gender-fluid, nonbinary, transgender, and more. Forget about "sex before marriage is a sin," Nico was my window into this whole new world and a generation that spoke a different language. They were just an open book, and my trusted translator, allowing me to ask dumb questions (much like Stephanie had when I first met her). I just love them forever.

We made it to Galway, where we walked through the streets and ate crepes. And then we decided to go see the supposedly stunning views and rocky terrain of the Cliffs of Moher. It was a drizzly day, and by the time we arrived, the fog had rolled in so we couldn't see a thing. It didn't matter: we took pictures of ourselves and danced in the fog and had an incredible bonding day.

I think I learned the most from Miriam. She is a master actor, always making nuanced, smart, and incredibly funny choices as Diana. But my favorite thing was watching her as a director. She helmed two episodes and had complete command on set; she always knew how to give you the best note to convey the scene. (Fun fact: She also went to the University of Michigan with Hunter, and they might've had a brief dalliance, which we never really talked about, but Hunter's cute, so I get it.)

My favorite part of the writing process is finding all the narrative threads throughout my life, which is why crochet is such a good metaphor. Each blanket I have made over my lifetime tells a very specific story, including those that are not quite finished: the owl afghan, or that pink-and-white-striped blanket I started before Emily arrived. I think a lot about what it means to "sew in the ends" and how this book helped me do that. There is meaning in everything if you look for it.

Along the way, I've also had some revelatory conversations with my father. He moved up to New York to be closer to Hunter and me—and, ultimately, Emily. He now makes his hockey-puck burgers and homemade French fries on the weekends, and we have even planted tomatoes in my backyard together. My greatest accomplishment to date, other than crocheting a mosaic crochet rug, and finishing this book, was making a homemade Bolognese out of tomatoes we grew from seed.

When I asked him if he wanted to read the book to make sure he was comfortable with what I wanted to share, he said, "It's your story to tell."

I wrote this book to understand my mother, and so that one day, Emily will understand me. I wanted to piece together all the meaningful moments, like a quilt, to make sense of who I am, where I come from, and how I feel about those I love, in the hopes that it, too, will be passed on, another heirloom, like the penguin blanket, and the *BADASS* collage, and those copper cookie cutters, as well as the pink-and-blue blanket that Emily's birth mother made for her and that Strawberry Shortcake bookmark my mom made for me: all pieces that Emily might use to tell her own story, one day.

ACKNOWLEDGMENTS

To my mother, who encouraged and pushed me down the unconventional path. Who championed my independence. I miss you, and I love you.

To my father, who taught me how to plant a garden and encouraged me to keep smiling and to seek the light. And who was there every step of the way while I was writing this book, always willing to answer questions, no matter how personal or painful.

Daddy, I love you and am so proud of you.

To my brother, Hunter, who blazed his own trail, and to Jen, who has been steadfast by his side, I am honored to be your sister.

To my Aunt Mary Anne, for being my inspiration—well beyond baking and crafting. Thank you for all of the memories you shared, both bitter and sweet.

To my Great-Uncle Ken, who passed away right before this book came out. Thank you for being an angel on this earth and for being one of the greatest men I've ever known. May you rest in peace (1927–2021).

To my entire extended family, the Jacksons and the Fosters: thank you all for being a part of this story. Of my story.

To my agent, Mollie Glick, for believing in this offbeat idea of a memoir. And to my editor, Suzanne O'Neill, for allowing me to tell it. Thank you for pushing me and not settling for anything less.

To the incredible Liz Welch, who became a friend and also a therapist during this journey. Thank you for your unbelievable patience, gentle prodding, questions ALL IN CAPS, long phone conversations, deep dives, and complete rewrites. Thank you for your collaboration. For believing in ME as a writer. And thank you for helping me tell my story in a way I thought was just not possible.

Thank you to Patti LuPone for being

YOU. And thank you for saying YES when I asked for an interview. I will forever be your number one fan. And you will always be my north star.

Thank you, Stephanie, for always inspiring me, for being my sister in this life. For your unconditional love and support and creative championing.

Thank you, Megan, my sister and friend, for always being there, checking in, and being such an incredible friend and confidant.

Thank you, Julien, my other brother, for catching me when I fall and for supporting me when I stagger. Thank you for your endless love and friendship. I love you.

Ted. My husband, my friend, my partner. Thank you for sharing this life with me. Thank you for your unbelievable talent, your incredible gift as a writer. Thanks for putting up with this "newbie writer" and for being a tough but loving critic. Thank you for making me better and the best version of myself. I love you so, so much.

And to Emily. My darling daughter. I don't know how I got so lucky to be your mom, but I am so grateful to your birth mom for choosing me and Ted to raise you. She is an incredible person and so are you, my sweet Ems.

Thank you for being so patient while Mommy had to go "write her book."

I can't wait for you to read it, someday.

ABOUT THE AUTHOR

Sutton Foster can currently be seen leading Darren Star's hit TV Land series, *Younger*, which returned for its seventh and final season in 2021. Onstage, Sutton most recently reprised her Tony Award–winning role as Reno Sweeney in *Anything Goes* at the Barbican Theatre in London. She will soon make her highly anticipated Broadway return as Marian in the upcoming revival of *The Music Man* opposite Hugh Jackman in February 2022. The award-winning actress has also appeared on Broadway in *Violet*, *Anything Goes* (Tony Award), *Shrek*, *Young Frankenstein*, *The Drowsy Chaperone*, *Little Women*, *Thoroughly Modern Millie* (Tony Award), *Les Misérables*, *Annie*, *The Scarlet Pimpernel*, and *Grease*. Off-Broadway, Sutton has been seen in *Sweet Charity* (The

Pershing Square Signature Center), *The Wild Party* (City Center Encores!), *Trust* (Second Stage), and *Anyone Can Whistle* (City Center Encores!). She has toured all over the country for her solo albums, which include *Take Me to the World*, *Wish*, and *An Evening with Sutton Foster: Live at the Café Carlyle*. Additionally, she has also appeared on television in *A Million Little Things*, *Instinct*, *Gilmore Girls: A Year in the Life*, *Mad Dogs*, *Elementary*, *Psych*, *Bunheads*, *Royal Pains*, *Law & Order: SVU*, *Flight of the Conchords*, and *Sesame Street*. She holds an honorary doctorate from Ball State University, where she also teaches.